Dream Talk

Your Hidden Biography

Irene Martina

Clairvoyant and Medium

1st WORLD
PUBLISHING

Dream Talk

Your hidden Biography

Irene Martina

© Irene Martina 2008

Published by 1stWorld Publishing
1100 North 4th St., Fairfield, Iowa 52556
tel: 641-209-5000 • fax: 641-209-3001
web: www.1stworldpublishing.com

First Edition

LCCN: 2006940374
SoftCover ISBN: 978-1-4218-9921-3
HardCover ISBN: 978-1-4218-9922-0
eBook ISBN: 978-1-4218-9923-7

Dedications

This book is dedicated to my husband Ron and my dear friend Marilyn, for their unconditional love and support and for their belief in me. I am eternally grateful to these two loving and beautiful people; they never doubted my journey for a minute.

And, in memory of my maternal grandmother and mother who passed on their passion for dreams to me.

Special Acknowledgements

I would like to extend a very special thank you to Karin Lynn and Rod Sheldon. Karin and Rod have given countless hours and immeasurable love to the development of this book.

They helped to bring it alive with their inspiration, dialoguing and dream interpretations. Their passion, loyalty and insights have been invaluable.

I am grateful for their friendship and ongoing support. Further, I respect and acknowledge their commitment to the study of their dreams.

I am confident that you will enjoy their contributions, humor and special gifts, as you come along on this adventure of learning and self-discovery.

I would also like to express my gratitude to the following special people:

- My husband Ron, for his unconditional love and support, and for 30 wonderful years of marriage. He made it all possible. I love you, Ron.

- To Marilyn Avient, my dearest friend and author. I am grateful for her integrity, unwavering belief in me and for insisting that I am the best clairvoyant in the world. I appreciate her contribution to the editing process.

- To Bev Kennedy, my friend and favorite Numerologist. I am thankful for the many hours of editing that she did. I'm grateful for how she brought out the best of my creativity and writing.

≈ To Grace Trynchy, my office manager and friend. Her patience, hard work, great listening skills and positive attitude make office work fun.

≈ To my friends Penny Maday, a wonderful artist, Kathy Oleksiw and Maxine Kerr for their feedback and loving support.

≈ To the wonderful clients who attended my Dream Workshops and inspired me to write this book.

Finally, I want to say a special thank you to Dr. Wayne Dyer. I have admired, enjoyed and loved him for many, many years. He has a great soul and a great heart. He brings inspiration to everyone he meets.

I had the privilege of meeting Dr. Dyer, a few years ago, when he visited Edmonton. He encouraged me to write this book. I would like to thank him for his wisdom and wonderful teachings.

God bless you, Dr. Dyer, for all the lives you have touched.

Irene

Table of Contents

PART 4: CONNECTING THE DREAM SYMBOLS

PART 5: FEELING ANXIOUS?

PART 6: RELATIONSHIPS

PART 7: OTHER SPIRITUAL DIMENSIONS

Irene's Story... Why This Book

I am a third generation dream worker. My maternal grandmother had been passionate about the wisdom and worth of dreams. I was blessed to have had a mother who was intrigued with the language of dreams. She passed on her love of and fascination of them to me and encouraged me to study and explore their endless uses.

The door to my dream consciousness opened when I was eight years old. At that time, I had two recurring dreams that proved to be prophetic. From that point on, the study of dreams became a major part of my life.

My dreams have solved problems and helped me to connect with my guides and deceased loved ones. My dreams told me when I had cancer and other health problems. They gave me advanced warning, so that I could act proactively and better deal with those problems.

Dreams heightened my intuition and clairvoyance skills from the moment that I paid attention to them. For example, at the age of 19, I dreamed that I would move further west and settle in a city where I did not know a soul. Intuitively, I knew that this unknown city was where my destiny would unfold.

Two years later, I was on a train headed for the west coast of Canada. Due to a lack of funds I was forced to disembark in an unfamiliar city, Edmonton, Alberta. That was where I stayed; I never continued my trip to the coast. It was in Edmonton where I met my husband, my soul mate. And, it was there that I finally embraced my true calling, as a clairvoyant medium.

For a long time, I had been aware that many people were searching for a book that would help them understand their dreams. They wanted a "how to" book, rather than another "dream dictionary".

A major shortfall of dream directories is that they only represent the viewpoint of the author. They do not teach the dreamer how to interpret personal dream symbols. Nor do they teach how to decode the messages held in dreams. Many dream dictionaries contradict each other; some even contradict themselves.

My vision was to write a book that would teach the key concepts of dream interpretation. I wanted it to be informative, easy to use and appealing to all age groups. I also wanted it to be inspiring and empowering, to anyone who used it.

I chose not to repeat a lot of scientific data, such as the psychological aspects of the dream state or where in the sleep cycle dreams occur. Instead, I chose to share with you my knowledge, which is based on more than 50 years of interpreting and applying the wisdom of dreams.

My book is intended to help you learn and become fluent in the language of your dreams. To do that, you must understand your dream symbols and be able to apply the "grammar", orderliness and patterns of this new language to your dreams.

This book provides the foundation for dream interpretation. It includes the principles upon which dream interpretation is based and the techniques for understanding the information that has been garnered.

I hope to help you understand, from the perspective of a clairvoyant, some of the spiritual aspects of your dreams. These can be powerful and enlightening. I also hope to help you to get in touch with your imagination and creativity on a very deep level.

This book will give you the tools to understand your dreams and to have fun in the process. The application and worth of some of those tools are demonstrated, most notably in the dream dialogue discussions and exercises.

I would like to point out that every dream in this book is real. They were all experienced by my clients, colleagues, friends or me.

Everyone is born with a powerful gift—the ability to dream. Through dreams you can receive guidance and answers to questions; these can direct your life.

You may overlook or disregard your dreams; why do you do this? Perhaps it's because they are confusing or frustrating. Dreams are not logical. The language of dreams is made up of symbols and metaphors, which are unique to the dreamer. Thus, *dreaming is a highly personal experience.*

I have worked with clients for many years, both in dream workshops and in private dream consultations. I have shown those clients how to discover the meanings behind their dream symbols. This enabled them to understand and interpret their dreams and to access their inner wisdom.

You may think that it will take a lot of time and effort before you can understand your dreams. That isn't necessarily true. The key concepts can be quickly grasped. After that, continued practice will heighten your interpretive abilities.

There is no such thing as a coincidence. If you are wandering through the pages of this book, it is not by accident. You have chosen this book for a reason. You are ready to learn how to interpret the messages that your soul sends to you, through your dreams.

Let's begin!

Part I: Using the Keys

The Power of Dreams

Dreaming is part of your life, from the time you are born until you die. Everybody dreams, from the youngest child to the most mature senior. Yet, few understand the meaning of dreams. Fewer still understand why these powerful experiences are fundamental for healthy, fulfilling and successful living.

In the course of your life—the crises, successes and failures—you may never stop to think that support, guidance, healing and renewed life is with you, in your dreams.

During the most difficult times, despair often obscures the most immediate sources of help. When you are "flying high", your elation often discounts the need for any power except your own. In both extremes, your dreams can provide you with insight and assistance, if you let them.

Dreams are a universal channel through which you have access to extraordinary guidance and healing. Dreams connect you to your guides and the spiritual dimension, which exist beyond your normal waking consciousness.

Everyone is born with at least two spirit guides; they are with you at all times. The entities and powers that reside in the spiritual dimensions can manifest themselves and communicate with you through your dreams.

Your challenge is to still your mind sufficiently, so that you can hear the "voices" of those guides. It is also for you to carefully consider their messages.

Dreams are like personal compasses. They communicate knowledge about your life, in all its dimensions—the physical, intellectual, emotional and spiritual. Dreams provide choices and give you a glimpse of what lies ahead. They offer direction to help you to shape your life, in the four dimensions.

Dreams are the soul's medicine, for healing the body, mind, emotions and spirit. Just as each soul is unique, the images, symbols and messages in dreams are also unique. Understanding and interpreting the language of dreams creates a threshold, which can lead to a profound healing and transformation.

To understand this language, you must learn a new vocabulary. This new vocabulary will enable you to interpret the meaning of your dream images.

Wonderful World of Dreams

Dreams have always played a central role in humanity's spiritual consciousness. For centuries men and women have searched for answers to their dreams. In the past, they have gone to: soothsayers, friends, mystics and perhaps even disreputable dream experts, searching for answers. Today, they still look for answers outside of themselves, when the answers are truly within.

Dream interpretation has been handed over to experts, who claim to be authorities on matters of dreams. The majority of people doubt that they have the ability to interpret and understand their dreams. They believe that they need interpretations from a psychologist, psychiatrist, clergy person or other professional. That is not to say that these professionals cannot be of help. They can, especially when deep emotional issues or other troublesome concerns are connected to dreams. Still, most people can learn to interpret their dreams and benefit from those interpretations.

Dream messages often remain locked in the subconscious and people continue to be unaware of the healing power and messages available through dreams.

I have witnessed the power of dreams and dream interpretation. I have seen several children; teens and adults overcome multiple challenges, including social alienation, by working with their dreams. Overcoming those challenges enabled them to reconnect with society and their daily lives.

As a result of my workshops, many parents sit down with their children and for the first time, help them to explore their dreams. I have witnessed the revitalization of marriages, after spouses began sharing their dreams.

Dream exploration can help you to navigate your waking life. Once you understand the language of your dreams and begin to apply the principles of dream interpretation, you can have access to their amazing healing powers.

Building Blocks: The Master Keys

Over the past 42 years, I have conducted hundreds of workshops and interpreted thousands of dreams for clients. Through a lifetime of dream work, I have identified 11 powerful concepts, which I call the *Master Keys* to interpreting dreams.

I am going to introduce these keys and show you how to use them by interpreting sample dreams. Then, I'll suggest that you try them, so that you can gain a better understanding of their use and effectiveness.

1. You are the creator of your dream.

This is the most important key. You are indeed a very creative person for you to write, produce and direct your dream. Everything in the dream is

A Symbol is any thing that means something else. e.g. a dollar sign can mean money or good fortune.

Metaphor: Something is identified by another thing. Qualities from one are attributed to the other. e.g. saved money can be referred to as a nest egg.

there for a specific purpose. You must take ownership of the dream.

2. Every dream is important.

No dream is insignificant. Each shows you the essence and uniqueness of who you are. Dreams are gifts from your soul; they will not take you down any path that you do not need to travel.

Do not worry; dreams are there to guide you. The messages come from your Higher Consciousness. Even nightmares have a purpose; they hold important information.

3. The language of dreams speaks in symbols, metaphors and emotions.

When you are sleeping, you are in an unconscious state. Your waking self (ego) cannot speak to you, in your dream world, in the same way that it does when you are awake.

Your Dream Creator (your Higher Self) accesses personal symbolism to create dream scenarios. These symbols and metaphors will speak to you in your dreams. Use this as a guideline and you will find it easier to interpret your dreams.

You may dream literally, some people do; however, this is the exception rather than the rule. A literal dream means that objects in a dream are exactly what they seem to be.

Literal dreaming may occur because issues have been thoroughly dealt with on the mental, physical, emotional and spiritual levels during your waking life. Hence, your dreams will tend to be less symbolic in nature.

4. The meaning of the dream symbol is always what it means to YOU.

Because you are the creator of your dreams, *the symbols are uniquely yours*. You must always honor this principle when interpreting your dreams. The same holds true when trying to help others interpret theirs; the symbols must be meaningful to them.

For example, don't merely say to your friends, "I saw a fence in a dream, but I don't know what it means." Try to find a meaning that *feels* right. Trust yourself; the symbol is truly yours when you resonate with it.

One way to "own" a symbol is to detach from it. Stand back and try to analyze it; pretend that it belongs to someone else. This allows you a different perspective and often gives you the correct meaning.

If you really get bogged down, you can play a game that I call **The Planetary (or Galaxy) Game**. Pretend that someone comes up to you and says: "I'm from the planet Jupiter; I don't know what a fence is, please describe it for me". Happy to help, you might say something like: "a fence is a structure, usually made of wood or stone, which encompasses or encloses land; it acts as a boundary".

If that description does not resonate with you, generate others until something does. Once you have determined what the symbol means, examine it more carefully, in order to gain more information.

To illustrate this, let me use the example of the fence. Look at its characteristics. Did it have a gate? Was it made of wood? Was it run down? Was the fence the only thing in the dream or was it enclosing something, like a yard or a field? Could it have meant that you were feeling "fenced in" or needing to set some boundaries in your waking life?

The deeper you delve into the description of a dream symbol, the more clarity you will gain from your dream.

5. There is always a symbol of you in your dreams.

Lights! Action! Dream! Wow, not only are you the creator of your dreams—you are also the star!

From the time that I was a child, my spiritual teachers taught me that *the biggest thing in the dream represents the dreamer*. Thus, it is important that you always take note of the largest object.

Just as your persona is the biggest thing in your waking life, it is the biggest symbol in your dreams. Your personality must be identified or symbolically placed somewhere in the dream. In other words, it is all about you, whether you are waking or sleeping.

In a dream, the self can often be found as a car, a building, a field or another large object. More often than not, it will be symbolized by a moving vehicle, which represents you in your waking life. For example, if in a dream, you were driving a car down a road, the car would represent you. The road would be symbolic of the journey or road that you are on in your waking life.

Look at all aspects of the moving vehicle and take note of its driver. If you are driving, it means that you are currently in control of your life. If you are not driving, observe where you are sitting. Are you a passenger in the front seat? If so, ask yourself if you are just "going along for the ride". If you are sitting in the back, ask yourself if you are "taking a back seat" to something or someone in your waking life.

You may be wondering how to understand what the car means, if it is part of your persona. Well done, you're on the right track! If you will be a bit patient you will discover, later on in the book, how to interpret your dreams. Interpretation of an entire dream is where the greatest benefit lies.

Here is another example. Imagine that you were driving down a bumpy road, in a brand new car (in a dream). You were passing a beautiful, green meadow; you also were passing a few other cars.

The car, a vehicle of action, represents you. The fact that the car was brand new could be an indication of how you are feeling. In your waking life, you could be feeling self-confident, knowing that you are looking good and making a good impression on others.

The bumpy road could be symbolic of your life. It could mean that things are not running as smoothly right now, as you would like. Perhaps there are some obstacles (bumps) that are slowing you down.

Trying not to complicate matters, the meadow is actually the largest object in the dream and it is also an aspect of you.

The green meadow could represent abundance, growth, relaxation, peace, etc. It also could represent the things that you are striving for, such as a specific goal and its rewards.

Passing other cars (people) could represent that you are pulling ahead of others, in your waking life. You may or may not know those people. The act of passing could symbolize a goal-oriented and competitive nature. It could also represent relationships with your co-workers or friends. They may be moving more slowly on their journeys than you are on yours.

Are you starting to see the connections among the objects and how they relate to you? It is important to carefully consider the symbols; it is also important to analyze the action and all other aspects, such as the background, of the dream.

6. People or animals are not always "who they are" in the dream.

Typically, people or animals can be understood in four different ways. They can be:

a. Animals and people, including those you know, in your waking life.

b. Animals and people that you do not know, but who could be coming into your life.

c. The realm of spirit, this includes: guides, angels, totem animals and loved ones who have passed away.

d. Characteristics of yourself that are mirrored back through dream figures.

Each of these will give your dream a different meaning. It is important to ask questions about the people and animals in your dreams, in order to understand the messages that they are sending to you.

Who are they? Are they familiar or unfamiliar? What is their role in the dream? Is there a specific role they play in your waking life? Do they identify themselves to you or are they bystanders?

When familiar people and animals appear in your dreams, it is because you have put them there. Not because of whom they are in your waking life, but more so because of their characteristics.

Your mother may be symbolic of nurturance, your father may mean protection and your pet may represent love and loyalty. Ask yourself if these are characteristics of yourself, which are being mirrored back to you.

What about a stranger, in a dream scenario, who hands you a map or some other form of assistance? Strangers are generally guides; they are there to offer you some direction for your waking life.

7. The action in the dream describes the process you are living through.

Dreams usually include drama. By drama, I mean narrative, action and conversation. Things happen in dreams. Characters do and say things. Events occur in dreams and the outcomes, which result from actions, are often dramatized or exaggerated.

The action in a dream, tells about the experiences you are going through in your waking life. Those experiences could reflect how decisions are being made. Or, they could be about the patterns of behavior that you repeat or act out.

They could reflect events that you are experiencing now or will experience in the future. They could also represent things that you have experienced in a past life, such as a disease or a healing process.

The dream experiences could also be events, generated by others with whom you live. Those dreams draw you in and generate energy that reflects your waking beliefs, thoughts, emotions and actions.

In each case, dreams often tell you, the dreamer, about the results that are likely to occur. They can provide life-changing information, such as: "if you proceed with the following behavior, this may result in …" or "a healing process is underway; it will have the following results…."

8. Journaling is your dream biography.

Why keep a dream journal?

Dreams often have recurring themes, symbols and narratives. The easiest way to begin to understand those recurring themes and events is by keeping a dream journal.

Unless you write down your dreams, it is unlikely that you will get the full benefits from your dream life. Your Dream Journal provides a foundation for an in-depth personal interpretation of your dreams. It can help you to gain clarity and to more fully understand your dreams.

It can also help you to remember them.

It won't take long until you begin to recognize patterns in the way that you dream. Specific messages, from each dream, will soon be understood.

When dream themes and narratives change, you are being given a glimpse of changes that are taking place in your waking life. Alternately, they could be a memory of some past life event. Sometimes the changes are so subtle that some dreams seem to be repetitions of previous ones.

Keeping a journal takes a little work, but I'm sure that you will find that it will soon become a treasure trove of insight. Keeping a Dream Journal may even become a passion.

9. Questioning your dreams is a key to greater insights.

To understand your dreams, you must ask yourself questions about the symbols, action, characters, etc. This will help you to accurately interpret your dream symbols.

Asking questions is particularly effective when you are able to discuss your dreams with trusted friends or family members. Have them ask questions and offer observations about your dreams. Ask them to challenge your interpretations; this will help to develop your interpretive abilities.

The most effective way to question your dreams is to ask basic questions of the symbols using the following key words: who, what, why, where, when and how? Later on, I will demonstrate the power of this questioning process through the technique of dialoguing.

Dreams are a form of communication. They are part of a continuous dialogue that you have with your Higher Self and the Universe. The communication flows both ways.

When you question your dreams, information, guidance and answers come from every conceivable source. Be prepared to receive insight from anywhere, no matter how unlikely or random that source might seem. Information could come from: your thoughts, the words of a friend, a song, a spiritual or physical experience or events that were foretold in a dream.

As you become more open to receiving messages, you will notice more synchronistic events and receive greater insight at an accelerated rate.

 10. Be willing to look at a dream, from multiple perspectives, when analyzing it.

Any dream can have more than one correct interpretation. Dreams are highly complex and finely crafted creations. They can have spiritual, mental, emotional and physical meanings, all within the same dream.

Past and future lives frequently add additional meaning that needs to be considered. Dreams of past or future lives may relate to your current life, but that is not always the case.

Dreams are never viewed in terms of black and white; there are always shades of gray in their interpretation. In addition, cultural consciousness provides other perspectives for assigning meanings to dreams.

 11. You can change your dream and by doing so, you can change your life.

That is a powerful statement. Can you really change your life or your destiny, merely by imagining a different outcome to a dream? Absolutely! Dreams describe the processes you are living and thus the likely outcomes; they are related. Dreams mirror your waking life.

By changing your dream, you change the processes you are living and consequently can influence the outcomes that you desire.

To change your dream, you must recreate the dream through meditation, visualization or self-hypnosis. Then, with or without guidance, relive the dream and consciously change the parts that you don't like.

It is possible to gain further information about the content of your dream, through writing about it or discussing it with others. Then, you can "go back into the dream", through the aforementioned methods and change both the narrative and the outcome.

I recommend that you do this for any dream that seems to have an undesirable end, resulting from the actions dramatized in it. Changing a dream is a powerful technique for transformation, both in terms of your life path and your day-to-day reality.

This technique can also be used effectively when addressing past or future lifetime dream experiences that are impacting your current life. The transformations may be very subtle; they may become clear only after a period of time.

You are your dream creator. *You can change, work with and apply the dream's messages in your daily life.* This is the true value of dreams.

Applying the Master Keys

The **Master Keys** provide a method for discovering the deepest meanings of your dreams. They will enable you to realize the full power of each of your dreams.

Reading about the keys is not enough to achieve knowledge and power. You **must apply** the keys to successfully access and use the information held in your dreams.

To help you achieve dream mastery, I have demonstrated, on the following pages, how to apply the keys. I have started with an example that I call "The Snake Dream".

Dialoging a Simple Dream: "The Snake"

Let's look at a dream with some very powerful symbolism. This is where you will see Karin, Rod and I in action, helping you to use and understand the keys. Karin! Rod! Let's go to work!

(Karin and Rod played a significant role in the development of this book. The three of us spent countless hours discussing and interpreting dreams. Excerpts from those discussions can be found throughout the book.)

A client phoned me early one morning, almost hysterical, begging me to interpret a dream for her. She wanted immediate answers to the following dream:

I got into my car and a snake fell out of the sun visor, onto my lap. I screamed and jumped out of the car. I woke up and felt very agitated.

What do you think this dream means?

Irene: Can I play Freud? He would probably say that, because of the snake, it was a sexual dream! Hmmm. But let's approach this by using the **Master Keys.** We'll start with the biggest thing in the dream.

Rod: That is obviously the car; so, that must be the client.

(Key #5: there is always a symbol of you in the dream.)

Karin: The basic symbols of the dream seem to be the car, the snake, screaming, the sun visor and her lap. And, how she felt when she woke up from the dream.

Irene: Woo! That's great Karin. How the dreamer felt is very important.

(Key #3: the language of dreams speaks in symbols, metaphors and emotions.)

Karin: The snake could mean fear, because most people are afraid of snakes.

Rod: It could symbolize some sort of mortal danger that suddenly appeared.

Irene: I like metaphors and puns. What about "snake in the grass"? It could signify someone who did something behind her back or someone who had betrayed her. Could that be what the dream was telling her?

(Key #3: the language of dreams speaks in symbols, metaphors and emotions.)

We need to look at the nationality of this woman. Was she from another culture, where a snake has other meanings? In some countries snakes are used in voodoo rituals. Snakes may signify terror or power. Or, perhaps a snake is a good meal! And, don't forget, the snake is a universal medical symbol.

Karin: Is the client a nurse?

Irene: No. I knew this woman; therefore, I could eliminate certain factors. So, I'll go back to my first thought—betrayal.

Rod: To me it was a betrayal, a betrayal that she didn't see coming.

Karin: I agree. The snake falling out of the visor was totally unexpected.

Irene: I asked the client which direction her car was facing; it was facing *east*. That meant that the sun would have been shining in her eyes, when she left her drive way and started to drive to work. That suggested that the dream referred to events that would happen in the morning.

The *sun visor* could have represented something that she was, or would be, putting down. It could also have meant that she would be "put down" by someone else.

I told her that something unexpected would take place that morning or at the latest, the next day. It would be a great shock, something that she did not expect.

Rod: The process she acted out, in the dream, was one of escape and flight.

(Key #7: the action in the dream describes the process you are living through.)

Karin: Then, she woke up with the feeling of panic and fear, and the need to get away from the situation.

Irene: Because the client was not in an emotional state to answer any more questions, or reach her own conclusions about her dream, I used my intuition to interpret the dream, for her.

Rod: Is that something you would normally recommend doing?

Irene: Yes, always trust your intuition, regardless of the urgency of the situation; it will never steer your wrong. I trusted mine, which I always do. I had to rely on it in order to quickly help my client, who was clearly distraught.

I told her that someone she was close to and comfortable with, in her waking life, would betray her in the morning, likely before noon.

The reason for this interpretation was that the snake was close to her; it was inside the car, not outside of the vehicle. I added that the betrayal could be work-related and that it would be a big shock.

There was a clue in the dream as to whom it might be. The clue was the sun visor. I took the sun visor to be a symbol, a play on the word *super-visor*.

Karin: So you felt the dream was precognitive.

Irene: Most definitely, there were many clues. The dream seemed to be taking place in the *present* (the morning) and there was tremendous *anxiety* and *a sense of urgency*. Emotion was a major clue. I also had a strong sense of knowing—that was my intuition at work.

Rod: What actually happened to your client?

Irene: She was fired that morning; the man who fired her was a good friend. She was devastated and remained in a state of emotional upheaval for several months. The unexpected event seriously affected her self-esteem.

Karin: So, what was the value of her dream?

(Key #2: every dream is important.)

Irene: The dream was warning her that something traumatic would take place very soon. She was being forewarned, perhaps to help her deal with the event, on an emotional level, before it occurred. She was being told to expect the unexpected. That was the primary value of the dream.

She later admitted, to me, that even though the dream and my interpretation had upset her, she went to work prepared for some sort of upset.

A second, hidden value was for her to always trust that messages are found in her dreams. She didn't do this; perhaps she will in the future.

Rod: The dream could have gone differently. She could have stayed in the car and screamed. Or, she could have grabbed the snake and thrown it out the window.

Irene: The fact she jumped out of the car depicted how she was likely going to react to the crisis. She was not going to confront or accept it. Rather, she would try to escape from it.

The emotional upheaval, illustrated by her screaming and jumping out of the car, caused her to lose connection with herself.

The dream had predicted she would deal with the situation in that way. It described how her life would be in that moment. She was thrown off balance in her waking life. It took her several difficult months to re-establish her sense of self and purpose in life.

Karin: If she had made a different choice, the dream would have ended differently. For example, if she had thrown the snake away, she would have been released or separated from the thing that caused her fear.

That would have given her more control over her life, after the events of that morning.

(Key #11: you can change your dream and by doing so, you can change your life.)

Rod: She also could have embraced the snake! Even after the events, it would have been possible to have gone "back into the dream" to alter her response to the situation.

Irene: So true. Embracing the snake or even staying in the car would have demonstrated more acceptance and control of the situation. That might have been the best way to change the dream. However, she was too upset to let me help her gain an understanding of the dream or to change the dream in any way.

Most people are unaware that a dream can be changed. (This concept will be explored further, in the section on anxieties and nightmares.)

By changing her reaction to the dream, she could have affected her waking life. Then, she could have reacted differently when she was fired and in the months following that event.

Karin: That would have saved her a lot of emotional grief.

Irene: If she had thrown the snake out of the car, she may have retained power and emotional balance in her waking life.

Rod: Metaphorically speaking, the dream was saying that something nasty was going to fall into her lap! It also said to be forewarned, so that the shock wouldn't be so great and it was suggesting that she look for alternative reactions.

Irene: That is right! Often, dreams tell you about who you are and what will happen in your life. They also reveal how you will handle—or not handle a situation. Dreams do not always give definitive answers. They may simply show you the choice that you are favoring.

Karin: So dreams provide an opportunity for the dreamer to ask: "is this the choice I really want to make?"

(Key #10: be willing to look at a dream from multiple perspectives, when analyzing it.)

Personal and Universal Meanings of Symbols

Keep an open mind about all dreams and symbols, and remember to assign personal meanings to the symbols in your dreams. *Personal meanings will be more accurate than those found in dream dictionaries.*

Also, keep in mind that with so many different cultures in the world, a specific symbol can mean different things to different people.

Dream directories are often based on the author's experience, culture and knowledge. In contrast, universal symbols are interpreted the same way, in many cultures.

Here are a few universal symbols. See if any of them match your definitions.

- Crosses: Christianity, religions, medical personnel, assistance (for example, the Red Cross), torture, punishment, death.
- Doves: Holy Spirit, spirituality, peace, weddings, freedom, purity.
- Rainbow: Good luck, abundance, new beginnings, happiness, and spirituality.
- Snakes: Fertility, food, betrayal, conflict, uncertainty, fear, sexuality.

When helping friends and family to interpret their dreams, remember to ask: "what does the symbol mean to *you?*"

Part 2: Capturing Dreams

Dream Memory

> Dreams are illusive and we must be careful not to lose them.

If dreams can be so profound, enlightening, prolific and powerful, why are they so easily forgotten? One compelling reason is that our daily lives are often stress-filled and exhausting. Our fast paced society has most of us falling into bed so exhausted that our dream recall is brief, if at all.

There are techniques to help you to remember your dreams; these practices need not add to your stress level. Dreaming can be as comfortable and habitual as brushing your teeth.

Dreams are illusive; you must be careful not to lose them. Stress upon waking or sleeping can hinder dream memory.

 The sudden buzzing of an alarm clock can instantly erase your dreams. Try to awaken slowly and gently; then as best as you can, recall your dream.

Take a relaxed approach to dreaming and develop a gentle, positive attitude towards working with and remembering your dreams.

Watch for patterns when recalling your dreams. Ask yourself the following questions, with the intent of discovering the best situations for dreaming and their recall:

   ⚜ Did I experience greater dream clarity and easier recall when I went to bed earlier and had more rest?

- Was the room lighter or darker than usual?

- Was the room temperature warm or cool?

- Did I affirm, prior to drifting off to sleep, that I would recall my dreams?

- Did I ask a question, to be answered in my dreams, before drifting off to sleep?

- Did I awaken with the answer?

- What was my evening routine? Did it vary in any way?

I was taught that dreams are gifts from your soul and that they are a way of understanding your past, present and future.

In order to recall your dreams, the desire to do so must come first. After that, you need to be willing to relax and assume that you will be able to recall them.

This approach can help you to sleep in a calmer and more peaceful state. This, in turn, can support your dream recall. It will also help you to recognize and work with lucid dreams. (Lucid dreaming will be discussed later in the book.)

A Dream Exercise: A Review of the Day

I would like to share with you a wonderful exercise that I use every night. It helps me to have clearer and more powerful dreams. I'm sure that it will help you to do the same.

Each night, before I go to sleep, I review my day in a backward fashion. The reason that I work in reverse is because stress and fatigue generally mount as the day unfolds. By working backwards, I can quickly clear away the accumulated stress; this helps to put the day's events into perspective. This daily review is similar to writing in a journal, except that it is done mentally.

I look for the great moments of the day, but I am also aware of the not-so-great times. The less-than-fun experiences often hold valuable lessons.

During this ritual I like to list the things, from the day, for which I am grateful. Sometimes, one of those things is gratitude that the day is finally over! That's okay; the intent of the exercise is to clear away the emotional debris and mental clutter, so that it doesn't appear in my dreams.

After the day's review and gratitude expression, I search for and identify my greatest learning, from the day. After I have given thanks for it, I allow myself to drift into sleep.

This exercise brings me emotional and spiritual healing, clarity, wisdom and peace. Additionally, my dreams are easier to remember and interpret. That's because they are free of anxiety that otherwise could have intruded into them.

I have found that by doing this exercise, it is easier for me to fall asleep. Not only that, the quality of my sleep is better.

What if You Can't Remember Your Dreams?

Some people believe that if they cannot remember their dreams, they must not be dreaming at all. That is simply not true! It has been proven, scientifically, that all humans dream several times a night, whether or not those dreams can be recalled.

A key to dream memory is *desire*. Do you want to remember your dreams? If the answer is yes, there are several things that you can do, to stimulate your dream recall and retention. Try the following eight suggestions.

1. Examine your nightly habits.

Are you watching television or reading something intriguing or stimulating before going to bed? Disturbing or vivid images and compelling information can keep you mentally or emotionally stimulated. This can interfere with your sleep and dreaming.

Are you getting enough sleep? If you are extremely tired and don't get sufficient sleep, exhaustion can prevent you from remembering your dreams.

2. Establish a calm and soothing routine before bed.

Meditating, listening to relaxing music or luxuriating in a warm bath can help you to enter a relaxed state. This will help you to enjoy a restful sleep and will encourage your dream recall.

3. Avoid foods, alcohol, caffeine and other stimulants before bed.

What do you consume before bed? Alcohol, cigarettes, tea and coffee can interfere with your sleep and therefore your dreams. Try not to eat or take stimulants before bed. Not only will you sleep better, you will dream better!

TIP: Drink a glass of water before bed!

A full bladder will probably wake you up, during the night, and force you to go to the bathroom. This will provide a wonderful opportunity for you to recall a dream. Rousing to go to the bathroom is less jarring than waking to the sound of an alarm clock. A gentler waking allows for easier and clearer dream recall.

4. Set an intention to remember your dreams.

As you drift off to sleep, state an intention that you will remember your dreams in the morning. Repeat this affirmation each night.

Please do not get discouraged if you don't get immediate results. You are re-training your mind; sometimes it takes time. Be assured that eventually, you will be able to regularly recall your dreams.

5. Record what you can.

Keep some writing paper and a pen beside your bed. If you wake up in the night, jot down a few keywords from your dream.

You do not have to stay awake and describe the whole dream. Allow yourself to easily fall back to sleep, fully confident that in the morning you should remember your dream.

> Karin: This really works! Even writing down one or two words like "bicycle trip" may be enough to stimulate your memory in the morning. The dream will flood back into your mind.

6. Wake up slowly.

Do not be in a rush to jump out of bed in the morning. Lie still for a few minutes and allow the dream to gently enter your conscious mind.

> **Karin:** It is important to capture the dream while it is still fresh in your mind. As soon as you wake up and start thinking about work, the kids or your "to do" list, the dream will vanish.

> **Irene:** Karin, you're right. Try not to let a "day thought" enter your mind. Try to wake up slowly, so that you don't lose the dream. If nothing comes, don't fret; just let it go. Your dream may return to you later in the day, when something triggers its memory. And if not, you are sure to have another dream that night.

7. Journal your dream.

Write down your dream *without* embellishing it. Do not write a novel! Allow yourself a few minutes to transcribe the essential dream. A lot of detail is not important; in fact, it can distort the message and interfere with its meaning. Logging your dreams will improve your dream memory.

8. Talk about your dreams.

Discussing your dreams can help you to decode their messages.

> **Rod:** Sometimes, I simply tell my wife the basic plot. It helps if you have someone to whom you can tell your dreams—a spouse, a friend or a co-worker.

> **Irene:** "Yes, it does help to discuss your dreams. Sharing dreams can often bring greater detail and deeper insights, in a shorter period of time

Dream Journals

The best way to recall, retain and work with your dreams is by keeping a **Dream Journal**. The practice of regularly recording your dreams is extremely beneficial. Some benefits are:

    Creation of a written record of your dreams.

- Enhanced confidence and knowledge in dream interpretation. The act of recording your dreams will encourage you to think about them. This will enhance your dream interpretive abilities.

- An exercised imagination.

- An awakened intuition.

- Establishment of the potential for gaining insight into your past and future lives.

- Identification of health problems, before they occur, so that preventive measures can be taken. Or, so that you can be better prepared to deal with them.

- Gaining insight into your subconscious, especially through understanding recurring dreams.

- Acquiring the belief and understanding that dreams are gifts from your soul. Further, that they can be spiritually healing.

- Developing a collection of written material that can be taken to a Dream Study Group.

- Documentation of precognitive dreams. This can be a wonderful validation of the accuracy of your dreams and of the gifts that they offer.

Try to think of your Dream Journal as a wonderful autobiography, filled with your life's magical and mystical adventures. After all, you wrote it and it's about you.

Key Ways to Enhance and Benefit from Your Journal Writing

1. Be factual.

A dream can sometimes be hard to describe. Thus, you may be tempted to make some adjustments when logging it. You must avoid changing or exaggerating your dream, in order to make it more coherent or more interesting.

Do not write the dream as you "wish it"—accept it as it is. Do not paraphrase it. Record it with as much objectivity and accuracy as possible; do not embellish. Changing it in any way will distort its message and result in an inaccurate interpretation.

2. Make Journal Writing Easy.

Use a hardcover or a coil-bound notebook, a three-ring binder, a computer—whatever works and is appealing to you. There is no right or wrong way to keep a Dream Journal, only your way.

I created a Dream Journal to assist you with the process of interpreting your dreams. For ordering information, please see my website: **www.irenemartina.com.**

3. Create a Dream Directory.

A **Dream Directory** is used to record the symbols, from your dreams and your interpretation of them. It is a wonderful companion to your Dream Journal.

Purchase a three-ring binder, with an alphabet tabbed index. It is easy to add sheets to the binder as it grows. Alternately, develop a computerized Dream Directory.

E.g. In Dream Directory: Indexed under Animals/Camel

(Additional information on creating a Dream Directory will be provided in the next section.)

4. Take Sufficient Time to Interpret Your Dreams.

It is important not to be too hasty when assigning significance and meaning to your dreams. Over time, you may interpret recurring symbols in different ways.

Allow for the possibility that new and different interpretations could come to you. Have fun with your journal. Allow yourself to fill it with question marks, scribbles, drawings, pictures and wonder! Be receptive to new ideas when they come to you.

Like anything worthwhile, the recording of dreams takes some planning and effort, but the results can be very rewarding! I am sure you won't regret the effort. Ultimately, you will be able to let your dreams guide your waking life.

I hope that your dream journal will inspire you to grow spiritually and emotionally. I also hope that it will help you to acquire significant self-insight and knowledge about your dreams.

> Try connecting your dream symbols in meaningful ways, to get the truest meaning from your dream.

Dream Directory: A Treasure of Meanings and Insights

A Dream Directory is a personal record/dictionary of the people, places, things and feelings from your dreams, and what they mean to you.

Keeping a Dream Directory will deepen your understanding of your symbols, whether they are delivered in dreams, visions or noticed in synchronous events in your waking life. In time, patterns will begin to emerge from the recurring symbols. This will enable you to learn more about yourself and understand what your dreams are telling you.

To get the greatest benefit from your Dream Directory, I recommend experimenting with the following suggestions:

- Use a three-ring binder, with alphabet tabs, because you will be constantly adding entries to your directory. This will allow you to easily add sheets of paper, as needed for each of your symbols behind the various tabs as your directory grows. Creating a directory in a computer in a Word Document or in an Excel spread sheet may work just as well.

- You will find a sample entry from a Dream Directory below. The sample dream is about green apples. I entered it under the letter "A" for apples. You could put it under the category of

"Fruits and Vegetables", if you find that more appealing.

Please feel free to use this example as a template, to create your own Dream Directory.

Current Entry			
Date	Dream No.	Journal Page No. *	Current Dream Symbol
April 21, 2007	*21*	*17*	*Apples (Green) were in a bowl on the table.*

Cross Reference to Past Dreams			
Date	Dream No.	Journal Page No. *	Notes From Previous Dreams
Aug. 15, 2005	*47 (2005)*	*31 (2005)*	*The apples in this dream were red, with brown spots.*

Note: * The Journal Page Number in the tables above, refers to the page in your Dream Journal, where the dream was entered.

1. What does the dream symbol mean to me?

Nutrition, health, harvest.

_____

2. What made this symbol stand out or seem important to me?

The green apples were really pretty and healthy looking.

_____

3. Does this dream have similarities to other dreams which have the same symbol?

In the other apple dream, the red and brown apples were over-ripe and going bad. They did not look pretty or nearly as nice as in this dream. In both dreams, the apples were in a bowl inside a house. .

4. What further meaning does this symbol mean to me?

I like fruit and I'm always immediately aware of it in dreams; I easily remember it. Fruit has always been symbolic of some aspect of myself; it represents some kind of personal growth.

5. What emotion is prominent in this dream?

I felt happy and content with the green apples.

6. Describe the physical aspects of the symbol.

There were six green apples in a pretty clear glass bowl. The apples were shiny and appealing; I wanted to touch them.

7. Was the symbol part of a dream sequence or did it stand alone in the dream?

The apples were the major part of both dreams; they seemed significant. I was not aware of other dream objects, so I knew that I needed to focus on them.

8. Could the symbol mean something else? Could it be a metaphor for something?

Metaphors/Puns: The apple of my eye? Or, the fruits of my labor? Wow! Perhaps the green apple dream was symbolic of growth and a happy outcome.

The red apples represented different emotions. The bruises could have meant that my ego had been "bruised". Or perhaps they represented some negative things, thoughts or problems that were eating away at me at that time

9. Can I associate the symbol, in this dream, with anything in my waking life (either recently or in the distant past)?

Yes. I feel really good about what is happening in my life right now. My relationships are good and my career is on track; it's "bearing the fruits" of my work. The other dream of apples occurred at a time when I was struggling in both my personal and professional life

10. If there were colors in the dream, what do I think they mean?

I like the color green; it is refreshing and it reminds me of summer. It makes me feel good.

11. Write down any additional observations.

I had forgotten about the other apple dream until I started a directory sheet for this one. I re-read it. Although the symbols are similar, the dreams are different. The mood and feelings, in the previous dream, weren't as good as in this one.

I will watch for apples/fruits in future dreams; I'll be observant for patterns and other similarities.

Sharing Your Dreams

It is natural to want to understand your dreams. The motivation for sharing a dream is usually because it has puzzled, worried or frightened you. Nevertheless, you may be reluctant to ask for another's opinion. Please do so. Sharing your dreams can be extremely beneficial. Two of those benefits are:

- Diminishing of negative emotions that are associated with the dream. Bringing the dream "into the light" usually decreases or eliminates any fear and confusion that is associated with it.

- Enhanced clarity of what the symbols and the story line could mean. Sharing dreams with family or close friends is helpful because they know you well. Often, they can help you to relate the dream's message to events in your waking life.

Dreams can also be shared with other like-minded individuals. In an effort to provide opportunities for such sharing, I started **The Dream Club**. It is an offshoot of my **Dream Workshops**. All workshop participants are invited to join the club and share their dreams with other members. (The club meets on a monthly basis.)

Each participant vows to maintain the confidentiality of everything that is discussed during the meetings. This is important because dream sharing means that personal information is disclosed.

During the meetings, each participant can share a dream if they choose while the others listen with respect and sensitivity. Then, the listeners offer their opinions on what the dream's symbols and message could mean.

A common approach to dream interpretation enhances everyone's enjoyment and learning. The meetings have proven to be a safe place for the members to deepen their interpretive skills.

You may wish to start a Dream Club. I suggest that you use the **Master Keys** and other information in this book, to help you with your analyses. Sharing dreams, with other like-minded people, can be enlightening, fun and rewarding.

Before going on to the next part of the book, I would like to say that I never make light of dreams. I always take them seriously, even when they sound bizarre. I firmly believe that dreams contain priceless information, which comes from your Higher Self. I consider it a privilege whenever anyone shares a dream with me.

Part 3: Symbols

Using the Keys: How to Ask Dream Questions

The language of dreams is made up of symbols, metaphors and emotions (**Key #3**). Dreams can be so rich in detail that you may feel overwhelmed when trying to interpret them.

When writing about your dreams, highlight the symbols that stand out for you, even if they leave you a bit confused. Try not to overlook the simplest symbols, just because they feel so common. Be sure to include your emotions; they are integral to understanding your dreams.

After you have identified the most important symbols in your dream, attempt to discover what they mean. The following 11 questions can aid the process:

1. What does the symbol mean to you?

Remember, you "own" all of the symbols. Ask yourself what the dream symbols may mean, in your waking life.

For example, if you dreamed of a rabbit, try to determine if rabbits have any significance, other than being a part of the animal kingdom. Do you or someone you know have pet rabbits? Do you like them? Do you have a particular memory associated with rabbits?

 If you still cannot determine what the symbol means to you, play **The Planetary (or Galaxy) Game** (this was previously discussed in Key #4). Describe the symbol to someone, pretending that he is from another planet or

galaxy; assume that the "alien" has no idea of what the symbol may be.

Describe the symbol's basic characteristics—do not embellish as this should reveal its significance. Your first words or impressions will usually get to the core of what it really means to you.

 In the rabbit example, you may describe it as soft, gentle, furry, cute, shy and nervous. You may add that rabbits make good pets and that they are very fertile and multiply rapidly.

Have your friend who is playing the role of "alien" keep asking you questions until he feels that you have given a thorough description of the symbol. By answering his questions, you will probably acquire additional insights about what the symbol could mean and how it could relate to your current situation.

Using the rabbit example, you might ask yourself if there could be some part of you that is feeling timid or nervous. You may also wish to consider if some part of your life is growing and expanding (multiplying).

2. What is the biggest thing in the dream?

Everything, every object and every emotion in the dream story is connected to you or is a part of you. This includes the biggest object, which generally represents your personality.

Be willing to examine it from different points of view. (**Key #10: Be willing to look at a dream from multiple perspectives when analyzing it.**)

Use this key, when thinking about the largest object and see how perfectly its principle falls into place. Then, identify the next largest object and determine how it relates to you.

 Imagine that you are in a field of daisies and beautiful trees. The field is the largest object; it is symbolic of you. The daisies and trees are a part of the field; hence, they too are a part of you.

They are extensions of who you are and they represent what is going on or being created in your life. These symbols may suggest that you are creating beauty (flowers), growth (trees) and strength (roots) in your life.

This dream scene could reflect the happiness that you experience with the beauty in your life. Remember, you must constantly ask yourself "what does each symbol mean to me?"

3. What are your feelings during the dream and upon awakening?

The language of dreams includes your emotions. (**Key #3: The language of dreams speaks in symbols, metaphors and emotions.**) Your feelings during the dream and when you wake up, can give you clues to aid in interpreting the dream's symbols and message.

A dream may start out as puzzling; proceed to anxiety and then move on to happiness. These changing states could reflect mental or emotional confusion that you experienced prior to going to sleep or during the few days prior to the dream.

Perhaps you were searching for an answer to a problem or a perplexing situation, before going to bed. Maybe, you asked yourself a question or two about the situation, in an attempt to elicit the solution through a dream.

If you woke up feeling happy and contented, you could assume that the dream's answer or solution to the problem was a good one. However, if you woke up feeling confused, you could conclude that your question was unclear or unfocused. It could also mean that the dream message wasn't yet complete or that it wasn't accurately interpreted.

Such confusion could suggest that the question needs to be explored and asked again, with clarity, so that the dream can provide a clearer answer. A clear and specific question is more apt to elicit a clearer message and response to a question.

4. Can you recognize the characters in your dreams by their looks names or attributes?

Three main categories of beings can appear in dreams. They can be from the physical or spirit world. These beings include:

a. Spirit Guides

In dreams, roles played can be by people who seem familiar; however, they cannot be identified as anyone from your waking life. Those figures are often your guides. Their role is to make themselves known to you and to offer some kind of assistance or support.

Imagine, in a dream, you were driving a car. In the seat beside you, was a somewhat familiar passenger. She handed you a map.

When you woke up, you could not identify her as anyone you knew. That person was probably a guide; she was offering you some kind of direction, as symbolized by the map.

b. Archetypes

Archetypes are symbols or imprints of a variety of personality types. They are derived from certain behavior patterns or characteristics. Those behaviors and characteristics are generally understood by a majority of the population. Some archetypes are:

- Goddess/Mother: The Goddess most often symbolizes maternal care, nature and fertility. It can also be a goddess of war and destruction.

- Healer: The Healer's role is to serve through healing of the body, mind or soul. The healer can appear in several roles and descriptions. These include a friend, a stranger and yourself.

- Hero: The Hero encompasses all that is good; the hero sacrifices for the greater good. It can be male or female. It can have flaws and become a tragic hero, such as Hamlet. It is courageous and may have extraordinary powers.

- Joker/Trickster: The Joker can be portrayed as the foolish one or as someone who carries wisdom in disguise. A Trickster often breaks the rules and is generally cunning, funny and different. The joker appears in many cultures; for example as a coyote in Native American and Aboriginal mythology.

- Shadow: The Shadow appears as someone who is flawed in some way. It can also appear as an enemy, adversary or despised person. Physically, it often shows dark features and can be of any race. It can symbolize conflict, complexity and one's state of mind.

🜚 Warrior: The Warrior typifies strength, and a strong will and spirit. He is a protector and fights for what is right and good. He is very loyal. The Warrior uses his skills wisely and does not fight for the sake of fighting, but rather to bring peace and strength when and where it is needed.

🜚 Wise One/Sage/Wizard: The Wise One is a spiritual teacher and can appear as either male or female. Her purpose is to impart spiritual awareness, humility and insights. She may appear as a kind, older, mystical mentor.

When unusual personalities (archetypes) appear in a dream, they are parts of you. These personalities should be carefully examined. They are not simply other people playing strange roles in your dream.

The source of the archetypes can be from within or from outside of yourself. When they arise from within, they represent parts of your character. When they come from outside, they represent roles that you have witnessed others play.

An example of an archetype in a dream could be you, as a hunter. You, as that hunter, could be seeking something.

C. Friends, family and acquaintances

As you create and direct the dream, you also add the actors to play out the parts. Friends, family and acquaintances are usually not themselves in a dream.

You generally place familiar people in the dream, not because of who they are, but because of what their characteristics mean to you. For example, Rod or Karin may dream of me.

They may think that, in the dream, I am symbolic of a clairvoyant. More likely, it's my characteristics, such as my sense of humor, my sweet tooth, strong intuition that is relevant or as a symbol of friendship. In other words, I am merely the symbol for something that they need to look at, both in the dream and their waking lives.

The previous example may show that they may need to approach a situation with a sense of humor. Or, perhaps they need to develop a "sweeter" outlook on something. Perhaps, placing me in their dreams is a message for them to trust their intuition.

If they see me as their friend, I could be symbolizing their need for closeness to other people. Or, perhaps I was in the dream to represent the psychic aspects of their personalities. As you can see, I could be placed in a dream without the dream even being about me.

5. Do you recognize the scene or objects, in the dream, as something from your waking life?

 Try to relate the dream scene and objects in it to your waking life. Something as simple as a tree, a road or a neighbor's house could be significant. Consider the possibility that those things could be related to your past. If you do not remember much from your past, consult an older family member or family friend. Ask him if a symbol could be something from an earlier time in your life.

One of my clients had been looking through her grandparents' photo albums. She spotted a house that had appeared in several of her dreams. Upon questioning her grandparents, she learned that she had often played in that house, when she was a small child.

6. Is there a sense of time in the dream?

Dreams can refer to your current life, a past or a future life. Try to determine if the scene is from the current time period or another century.

Do you get a sense of "déjà vu", a feeling that you've been there before? If so, try to determine if you can connect the idea, feeling or event to something in your current, waking life.

7. What is happening in the dream?

 Carefully observe what is happening in the dream. Then, try to determine if there is something in your waking life that relates to the action in the dream or to the dream scene. Look at the scene in detail; it may trigger some memories or lead to some insights.

For example, confusion in the dream could reflect something confusing in your waking life. Or, running in the dream, could reflect that you are "running away" from some issue during your waking hours.

8. Did you watch TV or read anything before going to sleep?

Scenes from what you observe or read, prior to going to sleep can appear in your dreams. If this happens, ask yourself if those scenes feel significant. Think about them and try to determine how they could relate to your waking life.

Imagine that you watched an action movie prior to going to sleep. Then, in your dream, you were part of an action movie.

Ask yourself if, in your waking life, you "need to take action" or understand some action. Do not discount the scene, just because it mimics the show that you watched.

9. Is a symbol really a metaphor?

Ask yourself if a symbol could mean something other than what it appears to be; it could be a metaphor. I find that metaphors and puns frequently give an immediate insight into the meaning of the dream.

Once a client asked me to interpret a recurring dream, which confused her. She often dreamed of railroad tracks.

Immediately, I thought that the railroad tracks could be a metaphor or perhaps a pun. I asked if she was feeling "railroaded" by someone, or if she needed to "get on track" with something in her life. The metaphors made complete sense to her; she was able to readily apply them to circumstances in her waking life.

10. What if the symbol has too many meanings?

Often, you can think of two or three possible meanings for a dream symbol. That means that there is more than one potential interpretation for the dream. That is perfectly normal.

Simply choose the meaning that feels right and fits into the dream story that unfolds, as you work through the symbols. Opting for a meaning that resonates, with you, can prevent feelings of being overwhelmed and indecisive. Those feelings could halt further exploration of the dream's secret message.

Even though, when interpreting a dream, you assign meanings to the various symbols, please consider revisiting the dream at a later date. At that time you may assign alternate meanings to the symbols. Revisiting a dream can give you additional insights and advance your interpretive abilities.

11. What symbols stand out the most?

Which symbols seem to be the most significant? Make sure you put those in your Dream Journal and Dream Directory. Those symbols can become invaluable for future reference.

Asking questions about your dreams is a wonderful practice. It demonstrates that your mind is awakening and exploring all aspects of your dreams. Writing your thoughts and feelings in your journal, along with questions can be reflections of that awakening. Greater self-understanding will very likely occur as a result of this process.

Understanding Your Dream Symbols

In this section I would like to explore symbolism and metaphors in greater depth. Then, I'll have you try some along with me. That will give you some fun ideas on how to dialogue symbols.

As previously indicated, a symbol can be an object such as a cup, pencil, song or book that appears in your dreams. The key is that the symbol means something to you.

Your Dream Creator (subconscious mind or higher self) communicates with you through symbols, because it has no voice. It extracts references, ideas and objects from your life's experiences and memories. It will only use things that you will recognize and remember or that will command your attention.

In your waking life, objects (symbols) also denote something specific. For example, a dog could symbolize loyalty and unconditional love. Thus, in your dreams a dog would mean the same thing.

You may be starting to see that dream symbols are not usually literal; generally, they are subtle and suggestive. A multitude of symbols, metaphors and emotions can hold a dream's deep message. Your initial assessment may tell you one thing. A second or third look at the dream may reveal its underlying (real) message.

Everyone Has A Unique Dream Symbol System

The best way to explore and understand your dream's symbolic language is by working with it. Part of this work involves writing down your dreams. The act of writing often brings clarity and insights about the dream's message. It also provides a log (record) that can be later referred to; this could become a valuable learning resource and a treasured piece of your dream history.

You may think that your dreams are scattered, random or even bizarre. You may be overwhelmed by the chaos, the sequences and symbols in your dreams.

A dream often unfolds in confusing patterns; thus, it is important to start an analysis at the beginning of the dream. Take one part at a time and slowly put the pieces together. The meaning of the symbols should be relative to the dream scenes and how they appear as a total picture.

You may reach a point where you feel frustrated and confused by the many possible meanings of each symbol. This is a normal part of the process; please try not to be discouraged. Continued study of the symbols can lead to enlightenment; that is a very rewarding part of dream analysis. The desire to fully understand your dreams is the key to unraveling their mysteries.

Keep in mind that an object (symbol) can mean different things to different people. Use your intuition when choosing meanings for your symbols. Those meanings must feel right to you and relevant to your dream.

The following examples illustrate some widely understood meanings for common dream symbols:

1. Airplane: This often means a journey, holiday or some destination. It can also mean prestige, speed, travel, business and striving for big goals.

Note that a plane is a vehicle, flown by a pilot. Determine if you are the pilot or a passenger. If the latter, it could mean that you are not feeling in control of your life. It may seem as if some other force or person is controlling you.

It could also mean that you are taking a passive role in some aspect of your life; for example, you could be sitting back and letting others "drive" you.

 2. Bird: This often signifies freedom, the soul, soaring aloft, complexity, peace, joy, or being part of a flock.

Observe if the bird is flying, sitting or swimming. See if it shows any distinguishing marks or characteristics. Look for anomalies and try to determine what they could mean.

A lame duck could mean that you are feeling restricted or crippled in some way. Someone or something may have "clipped your wings" and left you feeling helpless in some area of your life.

 **3. Computer:** This could signify a business, creativity, storage, memory, technology, your brain, work issues, vast knowledge and communication.

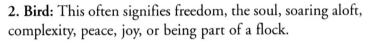 **4. Carrot:** This could mean good health, good eyesight or "dangling a carrot" in front of someone. If you do not like carrots, consider what that could mean, to you, in the dream. What could it mean if you love carrots?

 5. Chocolate: This could signify indulgence, a need to be rewarded, deserving special treatment, a fear of weight gain, a lack of sweetness or a need for more sweetness in your life.

Consider what it could mean if you do not like chocolate or are allergic to it. Conversely, ask yourself what it could mean if chocolate is something that you find very desirable.

As a rule, food in dreams are symbols of socializing, nourishment, needs and hunger. These things are a major part of everyone's life.

The food and its characteristics are important. When a food symbol appears in a dream, consider whether, in your waking life, you like or dislike it. Then, use that as a starting point for your analysis.

Karin and Rod are going to join me in doing some free association dialoguing to illustrate how different dreams symbols can be for each person.

APPLE

1. One word association:

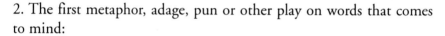

   Irene: Fruit.

   Karin: Harvest.

   Rod: Sin.

2. The first metaphor, adage, pun or other play on words that comes to mind:

   Irene: Apple of my eye.

   Rod: An apple a day keeps the doctor away.

   Karin: One rotten apple spoils the whole bin.

3. Personal associations:

   Irene: What if you owned an apple orchard? That could mean work.

   Karin: My grandmother had an apple orchard, so it could mean my grandmother's place.

   Rod: I think of the apple in the story of William Tell. It could represent a goal or a threat.

   Irene: An apple has a peel. Is there something that you need to peel away, so that you can get to the fruit of your labors?

   Rod: It can have "appeal"—something very attractive.

   Karin: I guess it depends if you like apples or not. What if you're allergic to them?

Rod: Could a person dream of an apple if he did not know what it was?

Karin: Good question. Can we recognize the symbols in our dreams?

Irene: Absolutely. Your higher self and your guides will only send messages in symbols that you will understand. That is why journaling is so important. It helps you to get to the heart of what a symbol really means to you.

Even though there is significant universal symbolism of the apple, each person will have a unique interpretation of what it means.

Now are you getting the idea? An apple could mean many different things. What does it mean to you? Shall we try one more?

BANK

1. One word association:

    Irene: Security.

    Karin: Money.

    Rod: Transaction.

2. The first metaphor, adage, pun or other play on words that comes to mind:

    Irene: You can bank on it.

    Rod: Take that to the bank.

    Karin: Robbing the bank.

3. Personal associations:

    Irene: Are you feeling overdrawn? Is your life balanced? Is life a series of debits and credits? Is your credit bad or good?

    Karin: What if you work in a bank? It could signify corporate business, management or your career.

Rod: Maybe you are worried about debts. It could mean loans, payments, troubles and obstacles.

As you can see, the possibilities are endless. Usually, the first thing that comes to mind, when analyzing symbols, is the most accurate interpretation. That is your intuition at work; trust it. The more you trust it, the stronger it will become. When a symbol's meaning *feels* right, use it until you resonate with something else.

Try the following words in the chart below, using the same format that we have just used. See what you come up with. You may wish to use it when developing your Dream Directory.

Symbol	One Word Associations	Metaphors, Adages orPlays-on-Words	Personal Associations
Clock			
Climbing			
Vehicle			

A Deeper Look at Symbols

As previously suggested, there can be multiple "layers" and meanings of dreams and their symbols. Analyzing the dream from multiple perspectives is helpful when searching for its deepest meaning (**Key #10**).

The dream analysis that follows is intended to help you deepen your understanding of symbols.

 You drop your purse. The contents spill out onto the floor. The purse strap is broken when you pick it up. You are anxious and wake up.

In this scenario, the symbols are: the purse, the purse strap, the contents and the floor. This short dream scenario is packed with information. What do the symbols mean to you?

In most dreams, you would be the largest object; in this dream, that would be the floor. However, because the floor is not prominent in this case, you would be the purse. The reason is because the purse is the focal point of the dream. The purse represents an action that involves you or is happening to you. Its contents represent various aspects of you.

You would still relate yourself to the floor as a whole. The floor could also represent the world around you.

Initially, symbol interpretation may seem to be very easy. It can be, but it can also be quite complex. A more sophisticated method of interpretation considers the *physical, mental, emotional and spiritual* aspects of the symbols.

1. Physical Aspects.

You drop your purse. Remember that the purse symbolizes you.

The action in a dream can often be overshadowed by the most obvious symbol; in this case, the purse. It is important to remember that there are more things to consider, in a dream, than just the objects.

Could the act of dropping your purse be reflective of your feelings? Perhaps you are feeling that things seem to be slipping away from you, either at home or at work, or both. Could there be a part of you that is stumbling or feeling unsure of yourself?

Perhaps the purse is a metaphor. It could represent that you have "dropped the ball" (dropped the purse) in some area of your waking life.

It can be helpful to describe the main objects (symbols) in a dream. Begin by asking yourself a basic question: "what is a purse"? The process of describing it can reveal its meaning. To illustrate this, consider the following description.

A purse is an object that is usually carried by a woman. It holds her wallet, keys, makeup, identification and other things. A purse can be made of fabric, leather, beads, straw or vinyl. It can be of various sizes.

You can expand on the symbol's description by asking yourself questions, such as those that follow. What are the physical attributes of the purse? Was the purse new, or old and familiar? What does the action of dropping the purse mean? Must a purse match your outfit?

The purse and the action of dropping it could reflect some insecurity, threat or uncertainty, in your waking life, at the time of the dream. I will explore this in the next section.

2. Mental Aspects.

The purse. Your thoughts give clues about how to interpret the scenario, from a mental perspective.

On a mental level, what would losing a purse (or wallet) mean to you? What went through your mind when you read the dream scenario?

Think about what a purse means to you. Consider if it could symbolize a personal value or your self-worth. If it does, ask yourself if you have recently lost some sense of value or self-worth in your waking life.

Spilling of the purse was an unexpected event. No doubt it would have caused a reflexive physical reaction. An attempt to grab the purse and its contents would have been a typical response.

Think about the spilling and the grabbing actions and try to relate them to your life. Consider if something unexpected happened in some part of your waking life. How did you react to it? Was it an immediate and reflexive response?

Did your reaction cause you to think or behave differently about something? Ask yourself if you need to "grab" at something, for example, an opportunity that an unexpected event recently offered you.

As you can see, assessing the dream from a mental perspective can generate many possible meanings and messages.

3. Emotional Aspects.

The contents spill out onto the floor. Purse contents are generally private; yet, suddenly they were on the floor, in plain view. What could that mean? How would you feel if you experienced this dream? Or, if the event happened in your waking life, how would you feel?

Because the purse is part of the dreamer, so too are the contents that spilled out of it. It would be helpful to try and determine what that could mean, from an emotional perspective.

Look at your waking life, for some unexpected event that may have upset you on an emotional level. Try to determine if it made you feel vulnerable or "on display" (contents of the purse on the floor).

Spilling personal items could have symbolized that you "spilled" some private part of yourself in public. The broken purse strap signified that you didn't expect it to happen. Thus, you felt exposed and possibly embarrassed.

If you place a high value on the purse (you) and its contents, which reflect your inner self, then consider if something has damaged your sense of worth.

Consider if you have taken emotional risks, in one or more of your relationships. Did they make you feel vulnerable?

Your reaction to all of these questions may help you determine what the symbols mean, from an emotional perspective.

4. Spiritual Aspects.

The purse strap is broken, when you pick it up. You are anxious and wake up. Although this illustrates both the physical and emotional aspects of the dream, I am going to place it in this category. The reason is to illustrate how a spiritual message can be part of the whole dream scene. I believe that the spiritual aspect of a dream can be the most profound and important part.

The suddenly broken purse strap could represent a part of the dreamer's identity that has been abruptly disconnected or damaged. That could result in feelings of being alone, fragile or vulnerable.

The strap connected the purse and its contents to the dreamer; that could have symbolized an important relationship in her waking life.

The strap suddenly broke. That action could have symbolized a severed relationship in the dreamer's waking life; for example, a recent death of a family member or close friend. The dreamer could have felt an abrupt disconnection to that person.

Some other event could have left her feeling disconnected to something important. For example, something could have caused her to question her spiritual values and beliefs. Perhaps, she felt disconnected to a higher energy source (God).

The dreamer should ask herself if something, in her waking life, had affected her security and left her feeling overly exposed. If something had, it could be the source of the anxious feelings that she experienced upon awakening.

The answer or clues could lie in the contents of the purse that had spilled onto the floor. Her values, self-worth or self-esteem might have been symbolized by the purse's contents. Perhaps she needed to consider if she was carrying "excess baggage" in her purse and thus in her waking life.

Take a moment and think how you might feel if you dropped your purse. A purse can represent your identity, security and persona to the outside world.

An expensive purse or conversely a cheap, shabby purse could reflect the value that you place on yourself. It could also reflect the opinions of others, or at least your perception of those opinions.

I hope that you can see that this seemingly simple dream isn't simple at all. When it is examined from the physical, mental, emotion and spiritual perspectives, significant information is revealed.

Learning to ask detailed questions about your dream symbols can uncover a wealth of information. This can lead to more insightful interpretations of your dreams.

Keeping a Dream Journal ((Key #8): **Journaling is your dream biography.**) will help you to more deeply analyze your dreams. Please do not let the work deter you. With practice, dream analysis becomes easier and yet complex and intriguing.

It is amazing what you will learn and understand, as you continue your study of dreams. Your life is like a wonderful mystery. Each dream becomes a clue to discovering the inner power and wonder of your psyche.

The world of dreams opens so many possibilities. Among these are the ability to connect with your spirit guides, explore your past lives and manifest the things, in your waking life, that you've seen in your dreams.

I urge you to keep "digging" and asking yourself detailed questions about your dreams. This is central to decoding your dream's symbolic messages. This process can help you to discover a whole new part of yourself! That is what makes dream analyses so interesting and rewarding.

Dream symbols can have different meanings and significance in different cultures and religions around the world. That is one reason why it is so important to honor the principle that the symbol is always uniquely yours!

Part 4: Connecting the Dream Symbols

Dream Settings

 The setting of a dream is just as important as the main characters, symbols and action. It is not uncommon to experience several different locations or settings in one dream. Those settings may be logically connected or be disjointed, random and confusing.

The circumstances of the dreamer must be taken into account, when analyzing the setting of the dream. This holds true when analyzing any part of a dream.

Unfamiliar surroundings, in a dream, might represent feelings of loss or bewilderment to some dreamers. For others, they may signify a past life, a future event or a desire to travel and explore.

A dream scene, just like a setting, may seem bizarre. A dream can have disconnected and seemingly unrelated scenes. Those scenes can be magical or surreal; they can jump around to strange places.

Sometimes, a dream has no scenes. When there are no scenes, there is no background or clues to orient the dreamer to his surroundings.

There is a reason why a dreaming mind creates mystical or unknown scenes and settings. Those things, just like everything else in the dream, are sending the dreamer a message.

It is up to the dreamer to decode those images and understand the message. Activities that are part of the dreamer's waking life will often appear as part of a dream scene. For example, a white room could mean clarity or a clean slate. That could suggest that the dreamer has an opportunity to start over and create a different future.

Thus, when recalling a dream, it is important to remember that every aspect of it must be considered. The temptation to focus only on the main characters and symbols must be avoided. Please remember to include the settings.

I have listed, below, some common dream settings for you to consider:

- Oceans, beaches and waterfalls.
- Mountains and forests.
- City streets and parks.
- Countryside, roads and farms.
- Your home and your parent's home.
- Work places, churches and restaurants.

Here is another dream for you to analyze.

I was walking down a road and saw a castle up ahead. The drawbridge wasn't down; I couldn't see anyone around to lower it and let me in. I didn't notice the landscape around me, only the castle. I woke up feeling frustrated.

What do you think it means? Did you start your analysis with the castle? What words did you use to describe it? Regal, mystical, fortress and fantasy are words that come to mind. The castle could also symbolize strength, protection, security, a past life and fear.

When helping a dreamer find the best meaning of a symbol, I'll often have him state what he thinks a word means. This often helps him to relate the symbol's meaning to something of importance in his waking life.

To illustrate this, I will turn back to the words that I previously used to describe the castle.

- ﹌ Regal: High self-esteem, conceit and an unrealistic attitude.

- ﹌ Mystical: Magic, surreal and spiritual.

- ﹌ Fortress: Fear of physical proximity and/or emotional closeness, aloofness, obstacles and fear.

- ﹌ Fantasy: Not living in the real world, imagination, creativity and artistry.

- ﹌ Strength: Power (inner and outer), faith, self-confidence, feeling weak and in need of strength.

- ﹌ Protection: Fear for self and others (both real and unreal), feeling weak and vulnerable or empowered.

- ﹌ Security: A strong need for money, love or something else, feeling secure or insecure within oneself and/or with others.

- ﹌ Past Life: A message from a previous life and/or a past life itself (represented by the castle).

- ﹌ Fear: Real and/or imagined fear, fear of mental and/or physical threats, and facing a fear or huge obstacle.

Can you see how this process could open up new possibilities and help with the interpretation of the dream?

Although the dreamer didn't notice the landscape (setting) around the castle, it had to exist. That omission (not noticing it) could be an important clue to interpreting the dream.

The dreamer might have been so focused on the castle, that he did not notice anything else. He may have been doing something akin to that in his waking life.

Perhaps the dreamer was totally focused on a challenge and didn't have the energy for other things in his life. Or, maybe he was close to achieving a long awaited goal and didn't want to take his eyes off of it. If those things were reflected in the dream, it could explain his frustration upon awakening.

So, even though the castle was the largest and most compelling object in the dream, the setting must also be considered. The setting may be more representative of the dreamer than the castle.

﹌

The following excerpt from a dialogue, which I had with the dreamer, illustrates how a setting can represent the dreamer.

Irene: Do you think the road could symbolize your life's journey?

Dreamer: Yes, that makes sense.

Irene: In the dream, was the road rough and hard to maneuver or relatively smooth? And, do either of these states relate to your waking life right now?

Dreamer: I didn't have the sense of struggling on the road, but it seemed that I had come a long way. I was impatient to get to the castle.

Irene: Did the castle feel like a formidable obstacle that you had to face? Or, was it more like a goal or a fantasy?

Dreamer: It felt like something I had been trying to reach for a long time. That fits perfectly into my business and personal life right now.

Irene: The castle was part of you and part of the dream scene. Can you describe the castle in more detail? For example, was it run down, gloomy or overwhelming?

Dreamer: The castle was very attractive and impressive. I was looking forward to entering it; I wanted to explore it and meet the people inside.

I remember feeling tired; I wanted to get some rest. The inaccessible drawbridge made me a bit sad and frustrated.

Irene: If the castle represents a destination, in your business or personal life, the dream shows that this is an attractive reality for you. Furthermore, you are close to realizing that goal.

In regards to the closed drawbridge, could you somehow be blocking your growth or the goal? Could the method of opening the drawbridge, represent something that you have to do or learn about yourself?

Dreamer: Wow, I have to think about that for a minute. My waking life goal is close. Perhaps in some way, I'm looking for others to "open the bridge" for me instead of taking the final steps to do it myself.

Perhaps a fear of finally attaining my goal is holding me back. That makes perfect sense! I think I know what that may be.

Irene: Perhaps the landscape that you did not see is part of the key to opening the bridge. Or, maybe it represents something in your future. Could the unseen location or setting reflect doubts about something in your present or future?

Dreamer: I think you have hit the nail on the head. My mind is swimming with ideas! In some way I may have expected the goal to just fall into place when I got close to it. That's not what is happening. That could be what the closed drawbridge represented.

I think I have the big picture now—and the solution! Thank you for giving me so much from such a simple dream. Your insight is amazing!

I hope that the previous dialogue illustrated the importance of looking at the dream as a whole: the setting, action, scenes and symbols. Because of our discussion, the dreamer was able to put the dream setting, or more accurately, the lack of it into perspective.

The *missing* landscape was the "missing piece of the puzzle". When he understood what it meant, he was able to understand the dream's message.

Had he not been able to figure out what the absent landscape meant, I would have kept asking questions such as:

- Was the background in daylight or darkness?
- What would both of those states mean to you?

Daylight generally represents such things as: clarity, enlightenment, warmth, safety, happiness and peace. Darkness could mean: peace, quiet and relaxation. Or, it could mean: a void, fear or transition. The meaning would depend on the dreamer's emotions at the time of the dream.

Remember, that careful probing of a dream can reveal its deepest meaning. Don't give up!

Dream Senses

The hectic pace of day-to-day living can interfere with your sensual experiences. During your waking hours, smells are frequently in your awareness. The sensations of taste, sight, sound and touch often go unnoticed.

Dreams can provide you with the opportunity to indulge in a variety of sensory experiences that you may have missed while you were awake.

Can you recall a vivid dream that had a profound or long-term effect on you? Did it stand out because of a vivid sensory experience? For example, did the sound of running water or pounding feet awaken you? Or, did you smell an apple pie baking and woke up craving a piece of it?

1. Sight.

Sight is the most common and powerful sense that is experienced in a dream. A dream usually unfolds like a movie, which is being played before your eyes. It is common to be both the audience and the actors in the same dream.

You could wake up from a dream and remember amazing scenes that had vivid colors. Alternately, you may not remember the colors because you were so engaged in creating the drama.

Have you ever awakened from an intensely vivid dream and thought that you had received an important spiritual message? Perhaps you felt that a dream was reflective of your journeying towards a long held goal. Or, that in the dream, you were being urged forward by some strong desire.

In such cases, it would be prudent to take note of the strong visual events and objects in the dream. Record these in your Dream Journal in an effort to understand their meanings.

All dreams have a plot or storyline that you need to understand; dreams that are rich in visual detail and color are no exception.

2. Sound.

In dreams actions can speak louder than words, or so it may seem. Hearing and sounds seem to be less common, than visual experiences, in dreams. Nevertheless, you must pay attention to sounds.

Remember **Key #3: the language of dreams speaks in symbols, metaphors and emotions.** This includes the sounds, music, action and words that are taking place. Some sounds can be quite literal, such as a voice calling your name or speaking to you.

You must observe the action in dreams and be aware of sounds. A dream may be silent until suddenly you hear a noise, such as knocking on a door, a gunshot or the shattering of glass.

Consider if the distinct sounds could be trying to send you a specific message. Or, if an answer to a question could be in those sounds.

Sounds, in dreams, can be very real; they can even awaken you. At such times, you may catch yourself speaking out loud. That is because you are still engaged in your dream's conversation.

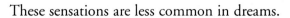

3. Touch, Smell, Taste and Temperature.

These sensations are less common in dreams.

Once I had a dream in which a strong, disheveled man was chasing me. He reached out and grabbed me; I smelled his foul body odor. The smell was so awful that it woke me. It took several days to clear the smell sensation from my memory.

Sometimes, dream scenes seem incomplete. For example, a scene could be taking place on a tropical island, yet you cannot feel the sun's warmth. Or you could be taking a drink of something, but cannot taste it.

Such experiences can be perplexing. They often trigger an awareness of lucid dreaming. Lucid dreaming will be discussed later in the book.

Dream Emotions

Emotions can play powerful roles in a dream. Sometimes, those emotions are not consistent with what is happening in the dream. They may be intensified, heightened and overwhelming.

Sometimes, when you wake up, you may have difficulty shaking the feelings that were part of a dream. Those feelings may linger on and mix with your waking life activities. This indicates that those dream feelings hit the heart of something significant. Regardless of whether the feelings were pleasant or not, it is important that you consider them when interpreting your dream.

When you are recording your dream, try to describe your feelings as well as the dream scenario. To help you with this, consider asking yourself questions such as:

- Do the dream emotions relate to anything in my waking life?
- Do those feelings remind me of anything that I have felt in the past?
- Did my feelings change during the dream?
- Did I feel more than one emotion?
- How long did the dream emotion linger after I woke up?

If the emotions are too difficult to analyze immediately after waking, it is okay to "put the dream away" for a while. You can revisit it at a later time, when the feelings have subsided a bit. At that time, you may be more objective and better able to understand what the emotions were trying to convey.

Another strategy is to detach from the dream. Pretend that it was a friend's dream, instead of your own. That may make the dream easier for you to interpret.

Rod experienced a dream with happy emotions. They lingered on as he awoke from sleep. He would like to share that dream with you.

I was in a Spanish gypsy grotto. I was looking for a spot to sit. Later, I got up and walked out. I met a little gypsy woman who said something to me. It struck me as being very funny. I started to laugh and couldn't stop. I woke up laughing.

Although there were many symbols in the dream, the most significant feature was the laughing. Thus, that is where you would focus your attention. You may even choose to halt the analysis there.

The dream could have been telling Rod to "lighten up" and look for the humor in life. Perhaps the message was simply to "not take this spiritual stuff so seriously!"

If you chose to probe the dream further, to look for other interpretations, you could ask questions such as the following:

- What does a gypsy grotto look like, to Rod? What does it mean to him?

- Was there anything significant about the gypsy woman? Did Rod recognize her as someone from his waking life? Did he recognize her laughter?

- If the emotions were ignored and the laughter suppressed, would the message have changed?

Rod's responses to those questions could provide additional insight.

Dreams can be healing experiences. They allow for the expression of emotions and thoughts that may have been suppressed during the day. Thus, paying attention to your dream's emotions can impact positively on your mental and emotional health. Conversely, by ignoring the feelings you could be denying healing opportunities.

Colors in Dreams

Colors in dreams generally do not capture your attention. Therefore, you may conclude that you dream in black and white; that is not the case.

Sometimes, colors stand out in dreams. Whenever that occurs, it is significant. Your attention could be drawn to an object that has an unusual color, such as a pink horse or a green sun. Or, the intensity and variety of colors could be riveting.

Just like any other dream symbol, color should be interpreted by what it means to you. It is also important to identify how it "feels".

Some people respond emotionally to colors. Others look at colors and feel nothing in particular; they could be "emotionally color-blind".

You may be surprised to discover that you intuitively choose to wear a specific color on a particular day. That is because you "need" the energy that that color brings to you. For example, red may make you feel energized and powerful, while blue may cause you to feel calm and poised.

The best way to understand your color dream symbols is to make them part of your Dream Directory. Then, use it with your Dream Journal. Together, they will increase your understanding of the roles that colors play in your dreams.

Here is a short exercise to help you identify your reactions to various colors. You may choose to put it your Dream Directory; it could become a valuable reference item.

What do the following colors mean to you?

Be spontaneous and work without preconceived notions; allow your thoughts to flow freely.

RED _____

BLUE _____

YELLOW _____

GREEN _____

ORANGE _____

PURPLE _____

PINK _____

WHITE _____

BLACK _____

The following dream, from one of my clients, illustrates the importance of color in dreams.

 I was in a store; yellow and black balls were falling off the shelves.

Irene: The store was the biggest object; hence, the client could be representing herself by a variety of "goods" that have value.

Karin: Did each ball have both colors or were they individually colored?

Irene: Each ball was one color; they were bouncing off the shelves, across her path.

Rod: Yellow is the color of the sun; perhaps it meant strength, energy and happiness.

Irene: I see yellow as a cheerful, happy and enlightening color.

Karin: It makes me think of lemonade; it is a warm color that conveys a sense of joy.

What about black? To me, black is nothingness, like outer space.

Rod: Black is burnout, a black hole.

Irene: Black is colorless. It's a void, an obstacle, and the color of death in some cultures. Some people might think of black as something sleek and classy, like a black Mercedes, a dress suit or a new cocktail dress.

Rod: Black is a dense color, because it absorbs all light. When you wear a black suit, you draw other people's light and energy to you.

Together, the colors suggest bees.

Karin: Bumblebees.

Irene: My first thought was cheerfulness, because of the yellow and obstacles because of the black. I also thought of obstacles because of the strikingly different colors and the falling action.

Karin: Sort of like road signs or construction signs, reminding you to pay attention to something. So, the client may have been receiving messages.

Irene: Would those signs have been negative, positive or directional?

Rod: Road signs are usually for your safety.

Karin: Good point. The balls were falling across her path, forcing her to pay attention to them.

Rod: In traffic symbols, yellow means to slow down and yield.

Irene: Black is like the pavement; it could have represented her path. She may have felt unsure of where she was going.

Karin: Bounce back, flexibility.

Rod: Could it be a game such as dodge ball, where she needs to dodge things coming her way? Or, could it mean to lighten up, have fun and play a little? Black could also mean licorice.

Irene: I discussed possibilities with her, like those that we have just talked about. She concluded that the balls represented strong messages that were virtually "in her face". She knew that she needed to pay attention to them.

Initially, the color of the balls confused her. But, after I asked her what the colors meant to her, she decided that the dream's message was to "lighten up". Yellow meant sunshine, happiness and fun to her.

The black balls were seen as obstacles, anxieties and stressful situations that seemed to be constantly "bouncing" her way, at work. She loved that image! She told me that the next time stress and problems came to her she would imagine them as balls and simply let them bounce away.

She was about to go on a holiday. She felt the dream's message was telling her to have fun, not only while on the holiday, but also everyday. Thus, the message in the dream was a gift that was intended to help her enjoy life. Discussing the dream helped to "unwrap" that gift.

In the dialogue, we discussed how the color black could have represented a void, licorice, death, a new cocktail dress or a sleek Mercedes. I hope that you can see, from our discussion, that the meaning of a color is a very personal thing.

A Dream Directory (dictionary), which has been written by another person, can give you some guidance and trigger ideas about colors and symbols. However, it cannot tell you how you feel about them. Remember that you must always assign meanings that feel right for you.

Part 5: Feeling Anxious?

 ## The Shadow of Dreams

I remember when I was about 12 years old, a neighbor telling my mother that she had had nightmares for years. The woman believed that she was haunted by demons.

The woman's dream is an example of how disturbing and persistent bad dreams can negatively affect a person's life. It also illustrates that cultural and religious beliefs can influence the content of disturbing dreams. The woman had emigrated from Europe; perhaps something in her background encouraged her belief in demons.

Anxiety Dreams

Anxiety dreams are identified by their distressing emotional content. These can include feelings of uneasiness, vulnerability, embarrassment or fear.

Everyone experiences anxiety dreams at one time or another; in fact, these types of dreams are quite common. Anxiety dreams help to release unwanted emotions from your waking life.

When they occur something may have overwhelmed, frightened or disgusted you at work or elsewhere in your life. For example, a graphic item from the evening news could be carried into your sleep and be expressed as an anxiety dream.

In all dreams you must look for the symbolism, anxiety dreams are no exception. Use the **Master Keys** to interpret anxiety dreams. Do the same when interpreting nightmares and night terrors (these will be discussed later in this chapter).

An anxiety dream can make you aware that you need to face and deal with some frustration or confusion in your waking life. A classic anxiety dream is one in which the dreamer feels tested in some way. For example, she could be writing an exam and not know the answers. Such a dream could be indicative of a fear of failure, self-doubt or being watched or tested in some part of her waking life.

Another common anxiety dream scene is one in which the dreamer is completely or partially naked or inappropriately dressed. This dream could reflect feelings of vulnerability, being exposed, embarrassed or uneasy in the waking state.

Falling dreams, which I will discuss later in this chapter, can often elicit great fear and anxiety. They generally indicate that the dreamer is feeling out of control or insecure, in his waking life.

Anxiety dreams, nightmares, night terrors and "normal" dreams all serve a purpose. Each one is trying to tell you that you must deal with something in your waking life.

Understandably, it is difficult to detach from the extreme fear that often accompanies anxiety dreams. Sharing those dreams with someone you trust and writing them into your Dream Journal can help. These activities can help to identify and deal with the related issue; that is, the source of the dream in your waking life.

Psychics, clairvoyants and others with highly developed intuition often experience anxiety dreams. The reason is because they often sense cosmic and earthly energy.

On the evening of the bombing of the World Trade Center in New York, I felt uneasy and had an anxiety dream. I woke up feeling extremely stressed, but didn't understand the reason. I turned on the television and saw one of the planes hit the second tower. Immediately I understood the source of my feelings and the anxiety dream. Several people told me that they had similar experiences.

Nightmares

What are nightmares and why do they occur? Nightmares are disturbing dreams which arise from fear, anxiety, worry and other things such as relationship issues and health problems. They can occur at any age. Their frightening content can often and abruptly force you awake.

> Nightmares force us to confront emotions.

Common sources of nightmares include: childhood struggles, money, geographic moves, being tested (exams), health problems, career, and relationship challenges (both real and imagined).

Most people have experienced nightmares at least once or twice in their lifetimes. I have discovered, through personal experience and from leading workshops, that nightmares are often spiritual dreams. Are you surprised?

If you miss or ignore an important message in a dream, it will recur in other dreams. If you continue to deny or misinterpret the message, your dreams may escalate in frequency and/or intensity.

Those dreams can develop into nightmares. Your subconscious mind uses nightmares to get you to pay attention to those messages. Paying attention to your nightmares helps you to resolve the issue that the nightmares relate to in your waking life.

In other words, nightmares force you to confront unresolved issues and inner "demons". When trying to understand nightmares, the first thing that you should consider addressing is any issue that you need to face in your waking life.

Your brain remembers every life experience. From the time you are born until you die, every thought, vision, experience, etc. is stored in your mind. This includes both the positive and negative.

In the dream state, negative emotions can be accessed just as easily as the positive. Fear, worry and anxiety are negative emotions and are often suppressed; that is, "pushed away" during your waking life. Unkind words and actions, that you regret, may be stifled; however, they do not go away.

Those suppressed thoughts and emotions can then appear in other ways. This can be physically (aches, pains, disease), emotionally (stress, confusion, doubts, fears) and mentally (lack of focus, fuzzy thinking).

Suppressed thoughts and feelings can also surface as anxiety dreams, nightmares or night terrors—any way that will force you to deal with the unresolved issue. Those distressing dreams are very common; it does not take much for them to surface.

Physical Aspects of Nightmares

Nightmares often have scenes of intense emotions and danger. The nightmares are allowing you the opportunity to express and acknowledge feelings that went unacknowledged during the day.

Did you know that your body experiences changes as a nightmare unfolds? Your pulse and breathing rate can double as you experience unwanted emotions.

Due to the intensity of those feelings, you could wake up in a cold sweat, screaming, trembling and frightened. You may even feel nauseous. The abrupt awakening is your attempt to escape the danger, fear, panic or other distressing emotion.

There is no denying that nightmares can be terrifying and seem very real. The after effects can linger for days. In fact, they can sometimes haunt you for years. When nightmares stalk, insomnia can result. You may be so frightened of the probability of experiencing a nightmare that you could be too afraid to sleep.

Living in fear and exhaustion can leave you mentally, emotionally and physically exhausted and unwell. Obviously, these are undesirable states.

If you have been haunted by nightmares for an extended period, please seek medical help. Sleep disorder clinics are located in many major cities. Smaller communities generally have doctors who can be consulted for help.

The following examples, of nightmares, include suggestions about their possible causes.

1. A Head Being Chopped Off.

Suppose you had a dream in which your head was chopped off. That would be gory and frightening. What could it mean? Here are some ideas to consider:

- Suppressed anger that is surfacing.
- Fear of something that you said and now regret.
- The need to face something in your waking life; perhaps a wrong decision.
- Mentally or emotionally "cutting off" some part of your self.
- A change of perspective regarding some issue.
- Dulled senses.
- A lack of life force (low energy).
- A disconnection from all forms of spirituality.
- "Cutting yourself" off from other people.
- Difficulty in reasoning (foggy thinking) or a change in your mental state.
- A rebirth in some part of your life, possibly in the mental realm; or something else that is wonderful.

2. Paralysis.

In this example, you cannot move; you know that you are paralyzed and you feel helpless. This is a very common nightmare.

Ponder the following:

- Something may seem "paralyzed" in your waking life, possibly in your job or in a relationship.
- You are feeling stuck in a rut.
- Something is holding you back.
- Fear of making a wrong decision.
- Impotency.

Pay attention to the part of your body that is paralyzed; that can give you clues to the interpretation.

Paralyzed feet or legs could represent a fear of moving forward in life. Paralyzed arms could reflect a fear of embracing or holding onto something or someone. Total paralysis could indicate that a deep fear has "stopped you in your tracks", in some area of in your waking life.

3. Death.

Dreams of death are quite common and should rarely be taken literally. They usually signify change, transformation or some kind of rebirth. Thus, death scenes can hold positive messages.

If you experience a death dream, please consider that something in your life may be ending. That ending will make room for something new.

Perhaps you dreamed that a friend, family member or a well-liked co-worker died; no doubt that frightened you. Such a dream could be an indication that your relationship with that person is ending or going through some kind of transformation.

If a co-worker dies in a dream, it could signal that that person will soon be leaving the company. Consequently, your relationship with this co-worker will likely end, or at the very least, change.

A dream of death could also reflect some kind of frustration or unfulfilled wish in your waking life. For example, a death in a dream could be reflective of an unsatisfactory relationship in your waking life. Perhaps you wanted to see that relationship end, but didn't have the skill or courage to do so. So, your subconscious mind helped you to end it, in a dream.

One of my clients phoned me about an upsetting dream, which concerned a death. In the dream, she was at her mother's funeral. My client concluded that her mother was going to die; naturally she was upset.

Intuitively, I knew that that wasn't the case and reassured my client of the same. Then, I asked her if a significant change had occurred in their relationship. My client replied that she and her mother had had a very rocky relationship, but had recently "buried the hatchet".

In effect, they had "laid to rest" old issues. Because the emotions were so heartfelt, they were expressed in the dream.

4. Being Chased.

This is, in my opinion, the most common nightmare. Being chased usually represents avoiding or running away from something or someone in your waking life. In a chase dream, you could be stalked or chased by a rapist, thug or wild animal. You could find yourself running in terror; you might wake up in fear.

You can easily halt the running, by "going back" into your nightmare and changing the action. You can do this right after you have wakened from it.

Picture yourself turning around, standing firm and looking the stalker (or other threat) in the eye. You may even choose to challenge the threatening being.

Facing the person (threat or fear) in the dream will enable you to more easily face that person or situation in your waking life. This can be a very empowering experience. It can enhance your feelings of strength and control. This will, very likely, halt the dreams of being chased.

You can also change a nightmare during your waking life. Find a quiet, calming and safe place; settle into a relaxed and meditative state. Review the nightmare and try to relate it to any worries or fears. Be receptive to your thoughts and feelings as they arise. Those thoughts and feelings could be messages from your intuition. Then, use your conscious mind to make any changes to the nightmare's action or outcome.

5. Being Alone.

Several people have told me that being alone is their worst nightmare. Dreaming of being alone is a very lonely and sad experience.

One client reported that, in her dream, everyone she knew had died and she was alone for the rest of her life. This caused her great mental stress and depression. Analysis of her dream brought her significant understanding and her nightmares stopped.

Some possibilities of being alone, in a dream, are:

- Feeling depressed or lonely in your waking life.
- Blocked friendships and trouble relating to people.
- Fear of intimacy or of sharing confidences.
- Physical or mental health issues.
- Being a bit of a hermit in your waking life and liking it.
- Needing time alone in your waking life and not getting it.

Look for other living beings (birds, animals, people, etc.) in the dream. If there are none, this could indicate feelings of complete isolation in your waking life. Again, I urge you to seek professional help if this type of nightmare is repetitive.

Remember! No matter what goes on in your nightmare, the interpretation must feel right for you.

Dealing with Nightmares

Not facing your nightmares can cause you to live in fear. As previously indicated, some people try to avoid sleep so that they can avoid experiencing nightmares. It is obvious that that is an undesirable state.

The most difficult part of dealing with nightmares can be facing them and trying to strip away the terror that they hold. Remember that nightmares are sending you messages about something that needs to be dealt with in your waking life. Nightmares can reflect unresolved issues, on a deep emotional or spiritual level.

Let me tell you a story about a participant at one of my dream workshops. She was an elderly woman. Her recurring nightmares had left her exhausted, physically, emotionally and mentally. She had been under psychiatric care for more than three years for the nightmares; the treatment hadn't worked.

Her psychiatrist encouraged her to attend my Dream Workshop. He wanted to see if I could provide her with another perspective on her nightmares. (I was delighted to learn that a professional was open to the possibility that a clairvoyant could help this lady.)

I invited the woman to tell me what was happening in her waking life, at the time of the onset of the nightmares. She told me she had just undergone a kidney transplant.

Her doctors told her that the anti-rejection drugs, which she was taking after the surgery, were likely causing the nightmares. Initially, she accepted that explanation, but after being on the drugs for a considerable time, she disregarded it. (Please note: I do not recommend that you stop taking any prescribed medication, due to bad dreams. Rather, I strongly urge you to discuss such a situation with your medical doctor.)

I asked the woman if she knew anything about the person who donated the kidney. She replied that the donor had been a thirteen-year old girl. When I asked if she knew the girl's name or her family's name, she replied that she did. As she looked at me, I saw the spirit of a girl beside her. I asked her if the girl had been Aboriginal; she replied "yes".

 I told her that the child's spirit was standing next to her and that she had a message. The spirit told me her name, which I repeated to the class; the elderly woman confirmed the name.

The spirit told me that she had observed the elderly woman suffering since the surgery. She wanted me to tell the woman that she was very happy in the spirit world.

She added that she wanted the woman to let go of her guilt and to enjoy her life again. She said that she would one day meet the woman, in the spirit world, and they would share stories. The spirit child told the woman to "live also for me".

The elderly woman wept with great release; the class gathered around and hugged her. She said that her tears were tears of joy, at hearing the young girl's message.

In the next class, the woman reported that the nightmares had stopped the night of the spirit child's visit. She stated that at last she felt at peace. She realized that she had been feeling extreme guilt about receiving a kidney from the young girl. She had been having difficulty in coming to terms with the fact that in order for her to live, a young person had to die.

To this day, the woman remains nightmare free.

Irene's Dracula Dream

I would like to share one of my nightmares, which had recurred for many years. I had had many nightmares about Dracula; however, this was the first one in which I had been his bride.

Rod, Karin and I will now dialogue it. I hope that you will be able to see how our analysis turned a horrible nightmare into a powerfully freeing situation.

> *In the dream, I was looking at a child, who was leaning against a picket fence. Dracula told me to go and suck the child's blood and make the child one of us.*
>
> *I looked at Dracula and said: "No! I will not do this any longer, I want to be free". Dracula replied: "you can never be free of me".*
>
> *I walked over to the child and was about to bite his neck. Instead, I impaled myself on a stake in the wooden fence; it went right through my heart. Then, I woke up.*

Karin: When you woke up, how did you feel?

Irene: I felt free! A stake through the heart means the mortal death of a vampire. By impaling myself, I demonstrated that I finally had the courage to free myself of him. I felt that perhaps I would be "reborn" into a new life.

Dracula had haunted me all of my life; that dream finally released me of him. He not only represented my fears and insecurities, he was my childhood demon—I will explain this in a minute.

Rod: So this was a recurring dream?

Irene: Yes. Many people have nightmares with a recurring theme, person or object. I'm no exception. Repetitive dreams and nightmares indicate that there is something that you need to face and deal with in your waking life.

Rod: What did you fear, in the dream?

Irene: What I feared most, in the recurring dreams, were evil spirits and meeting Dracula for "real". That fear was linked to my ability to see spirits. While dreaming, I thought that Dracula and others like him would come to me, just as benevolent spirits do.

I carried that fear of evil spirits from childhood. The dream could have been the manifestation of those insecurities and a sense of unworthiness. I had felt both so keenly during my childhood and teen years.

When I was a child, I had difficulty distinguishing between my imagination and reality, as do most small children. No one told me that Dracula didn't exist, so I didn't know any better. I realized, as an adult, that Dracula wasn't real. Nevertheless, the image was so deeply ingrained in me that I could not shake him, until I had the aforementioned dream.

Fear can cause you to abruptly wake up from a nightmare. I recommend that, after you have calmed down, you analyze the nightmare and try to determine its cause. It may help to consider the following:

- You may have been avoiding something in your waking life. What could it be?

- You may have built up an unrealistic fear of something in your waking life. What could that be?

- Facing the monsters or fears in your dream may help you to identify them. It may also help you to take control of the related issues in your waking life.

- You may think that you have identified the source of the nightmares but if they continue, you haven't. That is because the cause is buried deeply within your psyche. Professional assistance may be necessary to help you discover the cause.

Each dream and nightmare has to be examined for the symbols that stand out. Those significant symbols will enable you to zero in on the dream's message. Remember you are the creator, writer and producer of your dream. You must ask yourself *why* you created it.

Dracula had become part of my childhood fears; he was ingrained in my psyche. I knew that I needed to face him. Merely thinking or verbalizing that I wanted him out of my life didn't work. The fear of him was my issue; I needed to take control of it.

So, I impaled myself on the fence stake. I knew that I was demonstrating to him in a "language" that he could understand that I was through with his haunting. Indeed, that action ended his terrorizing of me.

Dracula had represented my "shadow" side. In other words, he symbolized my unknown or biggest fears.

He could have symbolized many other things. Perhaps he was my masculine power; he may have given me the courage and strength to fight when I needed to fight. Or, he could have represented a fear of authority and power. Perhaps he represented a desire for immortality. He could even have symbolized a fear that evil exists in the universe and that it could ultimately overcome goodness.

Rod: You achieved your freedom by driving a stake through your heart. That was like an act of love, it showed that you wanted to spare the child. The dream could have been telling you to follow your heart.

Irene: I believe that Dracula and the child were also symbolic of me. I needed to save my "inner child" and release my long held childhood fears of Dracula. I needed to reclaim my power.

The act of impaling myself freed me; in effect, I was reborn. My action meant that now I had the power over him, rather than the reverse. I had won!

Karin: So, what do you think the real message was in your dream?

Irene: The first thing that came to mind was that I had conquered a challenge, which had been with me for a very long time. That challenge was some kind of fear, worry or anxiety in my waking life. Finally, I was free from something.

The Dracula dream had been with me for most of my life. I didn't know its source; that is, I had no idea what had triggered it, other than a fear that those types of spirits could exist. I think that over time, he became symbolic of all of my current life fears.

I had always longed to be free of him. Finally, my subconscious mind came to my rescue and guided my actions in the dream. I reclaimed my power and was free of Dracula's power over me.

Typically, in nightmares you have no control over the fear or threat. To gain control and eliminate the fear, it is crucial that you examine your waking life. Look at it from multiple perspectives (**Key #10**). Try to determine what it is that you need to face and release. Ask yourself if something or someone is trying to control or intimidate you.

When analyzing my Dracula dream, I asked myself if something like a relationship or my business was "sucking the life out of me". Because of the time that the dream recurred, I looked at it from a business perspective. I wondered if Dracula could have symbolized my clients. Some clients were very demanding and expected more and more from me. That was very draining.

I looked at the other symbols and tried to determine what they could have meant. The fence could have been telling me that I needed to "set some boundaries".

> Nightmares can become self-fulfilling prophecies, if you continue to fear and worry about meeting your "demons".

The *stake* could have been the way to control a situation or outcome. The *child* could have symbolized my feelings of vulnerability and of being victimized by my demanding clients.

It became clear that my dream was telling me that I needed to take control of the situation. It also indicated that I was not without power or choice.

Some choices, like the stake impalement, may be drastic. But, they can (and did) provide freedom. I was able to examine and work on control issues, restrictions and fears. From that point on, I was able to strengthen my boundaries and not let my demanding clients take advantage of me.

Rod: In the dream, you knew that you were getting bad advice from Dracula. Could you relate to that at all?

Irene: There are always people who give bad advice or try to manipulate others. Those people may try to discourage you from following your dreams or taking control of your life. Sometimes, you give away personal power to those demanding and difficult people.

Dracula thought that I would never be free of him and that I had no choice but to obey him. He may have represented the people around me who felt the same way. Those people may have thought that because they were family or friends, I had no choice but to listen to and obey them.

Beware of people who tell you that you cannot do something. Also, be wary of those who consistently express negative thoughts such as "why bother?" Those people "suck your blood" and can drain you physically, mentally, emotionally and spiritually.

Dracula may have represented the shadow side of me that thought "what's the use; this is the only choice, don't bother trying to change; there is no way out".

I knew that there is always a way out. I made a choice to change my life. I had to follow my heart and do what was right for me. In the dream, I gave up my heart; I was willing to die for my freedom.

I did not choose the negativity that Dracula symbolized. I chose optimism and to walk into the light and a new life. I recognized that everyday I have choices, just like everyone does.

Every dream can remind you that you have choices. Dreams bring issues into your awareness when you are ready to make decisions. Fear of making choices can be one source of nightmares.

Look for similarities and patterns in your nightmares, just as you do for your "normal" dreams. Enter those in your Dream Journal. Eventually you will realize just how closely your nightmares are connected to your waking life.

> **If you give into the fear of nightmares,
> you unwittingly encourage them.**

Here are a couple of exercises that have helped me, and others, deal with nightmares. I hope that, if you are troubled by nightmares, you will try them.

1. When you wake up from a nightmare, visualize yourself back in the dream. Go back to the event that you'd like to change and do so.

I used this technique after I had a dream in which I was attacked, from behind by three men. I mentally went back into the dream, to the point where I sensed that the men were following me.

I turned and faced my attackers. I held my ground and demanded to know what they wanted. I talked with them and convinced them to leave me alone.

When going back into a dream, the visualization is yours. You have the power to change the dream, in any way that you like. You can dictate its outcome.

By facing the three attackers, I realized there could be three things, in my waking life, that I needed to face. Those three things made me understand what the dream was about. During the next few days I dealt with those issues; the nightmare never returned.

2. Visualize that an escape route will always be available for you, in any nightmare.

Tell yourself that whenever you are in a dream that you wish to escape from, you will always find a way to safety. You might imagine an open door, an escape hatch, a guiding light, a detour sign, a safety net or anything else that seems appropriate. Then, when in a nightmare, look for your escape route and use it.

Remind yourself that nightmares are simply dreams that are trying to get your attention. Try to take the nightmares to a higher level of awareness. You can do this by analyzing them and searching for a spiritual message. This can help you to release the fear.

Taking a dream out of the darkness; that is, out of a state of fear is a priceless gift to yourself. After the fear is gone, you can search for solutions to the problems which triggered the nightmare.

Night Terrors

A night terror is an extreme form of a nightmare. Night terrors generally occur in children, but adults can also suffer from them. Night terrors usually take place during the first two hours of sleep. Most often, they happen within the first 20 minutes of sleep.

Some night terrors cause thrashing and loud screaming; the dreamer may be hard to wake up. Sometimes, the dreamer spontaneously wakes up, terrified and often screaming. She may be disoriented for 10 to 15 minutes after wakening. Fear may linger for several minutes.

Just like nightmares, night terrors can cause physiological changes in the dreamer's body. These include a quickening of the heart and breathing. Sleepwalking can often follow a night terror.

Each night terror must be dealt with on an individual basis.

Remember to use the **Master Keys** to help interpret them.

I am now going to relate two true stories about night terrors, both eventually had happy endings.

1. Night Terror Number One.

The first concerns a woman who attended one of my workshops in a last ditch effort to end her night terrors. She was in a state of desperation. This is how she described her night terror:

> *Every night, for the past seven years, I've awakened screaming after about 15 minutes of sleep. I find myself clawing at my throat and wrists. I get up and search for my purse; then, I go to the back door and look out at the car. After that, I wake up.*

Can you imagine how upsetting this must have been for her, her family and her husband who was in bed beside her!

I asked if she had gone for professional help. She replied that she had sought help, many times over the years. Nothing had helped.

I asked what she was looking for when she clawed at her neck and wrists. She told me that she was looking for her necklace, watch and a bracelet. I asked her if they had a particular value to her in some way; she replied that they did.

I asked her why she looked out the back door. She replied that she had to ensure that her car was still outside. She added that she had to go through her purse to ensure that all of her money and important documents were there.

I suggested that some kind of fear or trauma had to have triggered the night terrors. I asked her about the events in her waking life at the time that the terrors started. She declared with amazement that no one had asked her that before.

I do not remember the details of her story but, in essence, she told me the following. One parent had died and the other was quite ill. Additionally, her husband had lost his job and her career was not going well. It seemed as if everything that represented security and status to her was being taken away.

Intuitively, I suggested that she was equating her self worth with her possessions and money. That turned out to be the case. Immediately, she understood and accepted that her emotional security had been threatened, when the lives of the people she valued were changing so dramatically. Her night terrors ended that night!

2. Night Terror Number Two.

The second story concerns a thirteen-year old girl. She began having night terrors the previous year. No one seemed to be able to help her. So, her mother brought her to see me.

I asked the mother to wait in another room, so that I could establish a bond with her daughter. I wanted to make the girl feel comfortable and safe; I needed her to trust me. I didn't know if she would speak freely with her mother in the room.

I asked the girl if she remembered the time that the night terrors started; she replied that she did. I asked her a few more basic questions, such as, did the terrors begin on a weeknight or weekend.

Then, I asked if she could remember anything out of the ordinary that happened at that time. She looked very anxious; then, she slowly pulled a diary out of her bag. She opened it to a specific page and handed it to me to read.

She had written that on a particular Friday night, her parents had been entertaining four other couples. One of the ladies must have had too much too drink. She made an advance at the girl's father; they were in the front hall. She kissed him and suggested that they meet at another time.

 At that precise moment, the young girl had been exiting her bedroom for the bathroom. Her room was located at the top of the stairs, which overlooked the front hall. She witnessed the entire event.

She was stunned and didn't know how to interpret the shocking scene. She had written, in her diary, that her parents must be unhappy. She feared that they would soon tell her that they were getting a divorce.

The girl carefully observed her parents for the rest of the weekend;

nothing seemed different. Nevertheless, she was frightened and confused.

She didn't know if she should tell her parents what she had witnessed. She did her best to block it all from her memory. That Sunday night the terrors started. Soon, they escalated in intensity.

I explained to her how the event that she had witnessed triggered her night terrors. She was able to understand and accept my interpretation.

She still didn't know what to do about her fears regarding the stability of her parent's relationship. After some discussion, the girl decided to tell her mother what she had witnessed. I invited the mother to join us; the girl and I told her what we had spoken about.

The mother was so relieved to discover the source of the night terrors. The daughter was equally relieved to learn that her mother knew about the pass made to her husband. He had discussed it with her on the night of the party. They weren't concerned about the incident; they had a secure marriage.

The parents hadn't known that their daughter had witnessed the inappropriate pass; and they didn't know that she was tormented about the possibility of them divorcing.

Both mother and daughter happily left my office. Later they told me that the terrors ceased the night of their visit to me.

In both of these cases, I needed to identify when the night terrors started. I also had to determine what was happening in my clients' lives at those times. I knew that some significant event or stress had to have caused them.

I trust that these two cases illustrate that there is hope for people who suffer from night terrors. If you know anyone who is experiencing anxiety dreams, nightmares or night terrors, please urge them to seek help.

Have them contact a medical professional or sleep disorder clinic. As previously suggested, sleep clinics can be found in many major cities.

Helping clients end night terrors and nightmares is among the most satisfying work that I do. If you wish to contact me about night terrors, please do so through my website: **www.irenemartina.com.**

The Body in Dreams

For centuries it has been believed that dreams, about the body, accurately reflect the state of the dreamer's body and emotions. Apparently, the great philosopher Aristotle claimed that an illness could be felt in dreams, long before its symptoms appeared in the physical body. I believe that that is true.

Emotions that are not expressed can be stored in the body. There they can manifest as stress, pain or disease. Fortunately, dreams can be release valves for unprocessed thoughts and emotions. Thus, dreams are a way for the body to take care of itself.

During sleep, the conscious mind is at rest, the body is relaxed and digestive processing is completed. Also during sleep, emotional experiences and thoughts from the day are "digested". That is why the subconscious mind can communicate with you better at night, through dreams, than it can during the day.

Your body routinely sends you messages about itself. If you live a hectic and stress-filled life, you may not pay attention to its warning signals. If that is the case, your dream creator may send you messages about your body through your dreams.

Those dream messages may contain powerful information about your physical and emotional health. (During your waking hours, your intuition tells you the same things, learn to trust it.) Symbols of illness seem to be exaggerated in dreams; the reason is so that you will pay attention to them.

Dreams can do more than just alert you to disease states. They can be vehicles for healing; it is possible to experience physical and emotional cures through dreams.

Dreamers have seen visions of light, angels, guides and other spiritual symbolism, during their healing episodes. Several students in my Dream Workshops have reported healing events.

Nevertheless, should you have any dreams that suggest medical problems, I would strongly urge you to seek professional advice. You can use your dreams, in conjunction with medical treatment, to help your body heal.

I have experienced healing through my dreams. I have sent my body healing thoughts and visions of vibrant health in my dreams. By doing so, I was able to make a cancerous lump shrink and then disappear before I had to have it surgically removed.

Karin also experienced a healing dream. Her dream was very spiritual, in that a healer (guide) was there to help her, when she needed it. That dream is described below.

> *I went to bed with a booming headache, which I did have for three days.*
>
> *In the dream, I was in a desert.*
>
> *I met an Aboriginal elder.*
>
> *He put his hands on my head, to heal me.*
>
> *When I awoke in the morning, the headache was gone.*

Karin's example illustrates an important point. Sometimes, what you see in a dream is exactly what it seems to be. No more and no less. There are no hidden meanings and minimal, if any, symbolism.

Buildings and Houses

Buildings and houses can symbolize the dreamer's body, as well as her persona.

The action, that takes place in houses and other buildings in your dreams, provides significant clues about your emotional, mental and physical states of being. Therefore, examining the various aspects of the house can help to detect health issues, sometimes years in advance.

A client reported this recurring dream about a house.

> *I would be outdoors on the right side of my house. I would observe that I needed to repair or replace some shingles.*
>
> *As I walked or sat in the yard, shingles would fall off the roof and hit me in the head.*
>
> *I would wake up with a bad headache.*

My client had the dream several times before she called me. I advised her to go to her doctor because of the seemingly urgent clues in the dream.

The house, that was in need of repair, told me that she was physically run down. Specifically, the *poor roof* pointed to the "top" or head issues. The headaches were a red flag, which suggested that something was wrong inside her head. Later, she told me that she had been diagnosed with a small brain tumor on the right side of her head. Fortunately, it was successfully removed.

When a house or other building appears in a dream, it is often the biggest object (symbol) other than the landscape around it. The landscape often goes unnoticed.

The house (or building) usually represents a structure; hence in this case the physical self. You must pay special attention to how it looks, both inside and out.

Its outside appearance represents your persona, that is, how you appear to others. The interior of the house represents your life and emotions, in the past, present and future.

If you are having dreams about a house that looks run down, that may be how others see you. Perhaps you are unduly stressed, low in energy or run down. If so, it may be a good idea to get a medical check up.

Building a house or other construction, in a dream, could be symbolic of building a better you. It could also symbolize success, growth and personal expansion.

Destruction of a house or building could point to low self-esteem or deep changes within the self. This could indicate the releasing or tearing down of old habits, ideas and thought patterns.

Whatever happens in a building is significant, especially if the dream is repetitive. Thus, it is wise to closely examine the symbolism and attempt to relate it to your physical self.

Below are some ideas regarding the symbolism of various parts of a house:

1. The Basement/Foundation.

This can represent memories, including those of your childhood. The basement can represent old beliefs, habits, wounds and other emotional baggage that you still carry. Items there can symbolize past issues. Basements are the foundations of our life and how are beliefs support us today.

Sometimes, the basement can depict past life memories. In one dream, I was walking down some stairs into a basement. When I left the bottom step, I found myself in a castle in King Arthur's court. Several of my clients have reported similar experiences.

2. The Main Floor.

In a dream, the main floor usually represents your current life. Observe exactly where you are on that floor; that can give you clues about where you are in your waking life. Consider the symbolism of the following rooms:

Kitchen: Heart of the home, family, nourishment, creating and entertaining.

Family room: Family, hearth, friends, entertaining, relaxation, comfort and intimacy.

Small rooms: Restrictions, privacy, intimacy, relaxation and secret spaces.

Hallways: Connections to parts of yourself and to other spaces, and passages in the body.

A hallway can connect you to the front or back door; this can symbolize the need to go out into the outside world. A hallway that leads to the bathroom could represent the passage to your bowels.

Hallways to your children's rooms can symbolize your connection with them. A hallway to the master bedroom could symbolize how you feel about the intimacy that occurs in it.

Hallways generally go unnoticed in dreams, unless they stand out in some striking way. For example, walking down a long, dark hallway could reflect that you are trying to find your way in life. It could also mean that you are unsure of what you want in a career or a relationship.

Conversely, a bright hallway could symbolize that you are focused and on the right path; also, that you are making good progress toward a goal.

Windows: Vision and openness to the world. Observe if you are inside looking out or outside looking in through a window.

Looking in a window can mean that you are focused on your self. For example, you may be working on your feelings, goals or challenges. Looking in can also be symbolic of inner reflections, self-discovery and the seeking of information.

Looking out a window can reflect your perception of the world and how open you are to the events and people around you. Looking out can also symbolize the desire to see what your future may hold. Observing a clear day and a smooth road could indicate an easy period, while rocks and hills could mean that challenges are in your future.

Windows are usually transparent and easily broken. So too can be your feelings and vision of present and future events.

Stained glass windows may be symbolic of religion, old-world views and seeing things through "rose colored glasses". They can also symbolize an unclear understanding of your present and an unclear vision of your future.

Sometimes, I interpret stained glass windows as being symbolic of an artist and his creativity. I also think of them as being representative of the old world or past life memories; this of course, is dependent upon other events in the dream.

Please note that the symbolism of hallways and windows is the same, no matter on which floor they appear.

3. The Second Floor.

The second floor is sometimes symbolic of your dream world and future goals. As bedrooms are most common on second floors; both can represent your personal space, intimacy, privacy, spiritual growth, personal expectations and a connection to your higher self.

Moving from room to room (on any floor) can represent a change of state, restlessness and feeling unsure about something. It can also symbolize exploration and a sense of adventure.

Balconies may represent seeking a different point of view on something. Openness, new vision and ideas, expansion and support can also be depicted by these structures.

4. The Attic.

This space can represent retirement years, contentment and the fulfillment of dreams and goals. It can be a place of spiritual growth, introspection and carefully stored memories.

Walls, in any part of the house, mean support; they are akin to your arms and legs. Old walls can indicate old problems and fears. New walls can represent problems or issues where you are symbolically "putting up walls". A dividing wall can be symbolic of two different sides or two points of view.

Stairs are interesting. In my workshops, I have discovered that about 60 per cent of the students believe that climbing stairs represents reaching for goals. Forty percent think that stair climbing represents obstacles, struggles and hard work.

Descending stairs almost always points to an easier attainment of something. As indicated earlier in the book, going down stairs can also mean going back in time, perhaps even to past lives.

As you can see, a great deal of generic symbolism can be applied to a house or other building. Feel free to use these meanings. But remember! Dream symbols are always unique; their meanings must always feel right to the dreamer.

Falling, Flying and Floating Dreams

These types of dreams are very common.

Falling Dreams

Falling dreams are self-explanatory; these dreams include tripping. The tripping and falling can be from any surface and from any height.

You may wish to consider the following points when interpreting your falling dreams:

- The distance that you fell.

- The physical sensations. Some dreamers have felt like they were falling through space, from the moon. Others have felt as though they had fallen into a void; they were so terrified that they woke up.

- The location of the fall; it could be from a ladder, down a hill, off a building or a cliff, etc.

- The actions around you during the fall, and your feelings about those actions.

- If you saw, as well as felt, the fall.

The majority of people find that falling dreams have negative feelings attached to them.

My sister had falling dreams whenever she felt unduly stressed. Job insecurity and uncertainty about her future generally triggered them.

She hated the feeling of having no control, while she was falling. She didn't know where or how she would land.

When she woke up, she would always feel unsettled, doubtful and worried.

Controversy exists about whether or not a dreamer will "hit bottom" when falling in a dream. The meaning of hitting bottom is also in question.

Some people believe that if you fall and land in a dream, the landing will cause your physical death. I haven't found any research to substantiate that belief. Nor have I ever experienced landing in a falling dream. I always wake up before I hit the ground.

Should you have a dream where you hit bottom, I strongly advise that you carefully examine your waking life. Think about your job, health, relationships, etc.

Landing, in a falling dream, could be symbolic of "hitting bottom" in your waking life, due to some kind of destructive behavior. This could include excessive gambling, drug addiction, alcoholism, etc. If this is the case, then I suggest that you seek professional help, such as with a psychologist or medical doctor, particularly if this type of dream is repetitive.

One of my clients constantly experienced falling dreams. Intuitively, I suggested that she seek medical attention. She saw her physician and discovered that she had very low blood ("falling") pressure.

Could this have been a "falling health" dream? It seemed to be; the falling dreams ceased when she began taking medication that normalized her blood pressure.

If you experience frequent falling dreams, it would be wise for you to attempt to determine the cause of them. The source may very likely be some unresolved issue that is causing you anxiety, conflict or hardship, in your waking life.

The following points may help you discover the source of your falling dreams:

- "Falling out of favor" with some one.

- Feeling ashamed or disgraced. Or, feeling that you have slipped or fallen in social status.

- Making a grievous mistake at work; that is, feeling as if you had "fallen down on the job".

Sometimes, falling dreams are experienced when the dreamer is astral traveling. The sensation of falling occurs when the dreamer re-enters or "falls" back into his earthly (physical) body.

Astral travel is the ability to leave (travel from) the physical body, in a spiritual form. This spiritual form leaves on a temporary basis, sometimes spontaneously, sometimes on demand. It always returns, unless the person has died.

Astral traveling frequently occurs at night. Often, when astral traveling I have found myself abruptly falling back into my body, in bed but awake. I never remember what caused the sudden fall; my astral journeying must have needed to end.

Sometimes, I wonder if a noise or other sound, in my bedroom or other parts of the house caused the sudden (fall) return to my physical body.

Astral traveling will be discussed in greater length later in the book. Now I would like to focus on another falling dream. It is a child's dream. It is important to note that children have powerful dreams, just as adults do.

> *A four-year old boy had a recurring dream. In it, he was "returning to the light".*
>
> *All he could see was a very bright, white light. It was so painful that he could hardly keep his eyes open.*
>
> *The dream always ended with the boy falling for what seemed like a very long time. He always woke up crying.*

Rod: How often did the dream reoccur?

Irene: The boy's mother told me that the dream occurred almost every night for about six weeks.

Karin: Do you think the dreams could have been near death experiences?

Irene: At the time, the child had been experiencing health problems with high fevers. For those reasons, it is very possible that they were near death experiences.

Rod: What triggered the falling?

Irene: I'm not sure. The boy was only four; he kept telling his mother that it was too painful to look at the light. He told her that he wanted to go to the light, but it was blinding him. So he'd relax and "let go"; then he'd start to fall. Perhaps it was a near death experience, but it was not his time to go/die ("go into the light"). Or, perhaps it was an astral travel experience.

The action of falling described what the child was experiencing. That was likely a rebirth that occurred because of his illness (**Key #7 : the action in a dream describes the process you are living through.**).

Another perspective is that, symbolically, a message was coming from the child's higher self. The largest thing in the dream was the light. The message could have been "you are the light."

Flying Dreams

Flying dreams are usually fun and very positive. They can be exciting, goal satisfying and daring. Often, the dreamer defies the laws of gravity and is able to soar above the earth, without the need of a mechanical device. At other times, he is in an aircraft.

Have you ever experienced a flying dream? What was it like?

> Gender plays no role in the incidence of flying dreams. Women report as many flying dreams as men.

- Was the flight smooth or turbulent?

- Did you land softly or did you crash and burn?

- Did you feel empowered while flying?

- Did you file a flight plan and go where you intended to? Or, did you simply fly randomly with no particular destination in mind?

- Could you relate the flying dream to something in your waking life?

Dreams of flying can be symbolic of "flying up the ladder of success" or "flying to heaven and other galaxies".

> When you remembered a flying dream what
> did you relate it to? How did you fly?

Various postures can be assumed in flying dreams. It is fun to contemplate both the posture and where the trip took you. Here are some common postures:

- Superman-style with arms straight ahead. This could suggest that you are "reaching for the stars".

- Airplane-style with arms at right angles to your body. This may mean that you are "spreading your wings" and soaring like an eagle.

- Flapping your arms, like a seagull flying over the beaches and oceans of the world. The flapping could symbolize your effort as you strive for new heights.

- Hands on hips, in a kind of Irish jig fashion. This could depict fun, creativity and an absence of seriousness.

Several emotions can be felt during flying dreams. Some common ones follow:

- Exhilaration and a feeling of well being.

- A feeling that everything is possible and "the sky is the limit".

- A sense that spiritual freedom is within reach.

- A feeling of being in control of your world.

- A feeling of empowerment: "if I can dream it, I can do it!"

Here is a client's dream about flying.

I had the most magical and remarkable dreamtime experience! My husband and I were entwined in a loving embrace. We were talking and flying above the ground.

We went higher and higher, in an upward spiral, until we were soaring together through the starry universe.

Irene: What a wonderful dream! This is an example of one of the most romantic and enchanting dreams that you could have about your mate.

Rod: It would be fair to say the client thought their relationship had reached a new level of intimacy or emotional stability.

Karin: Or, it could have been an indication that no matter what happened in her waking life, the two were soul mates.

Irene: Yes, it was a very romantic and wonderful dream in which she shared her life with a man whom she loved.

As dreams are messages from the soul, this might be symbolic of a future husband if it does not fit with the relationship the client has with her current one. Sigh... I can be the devils advocate but one must look at all aspects of the dream and its meaning.

But, let me play the devil's advocate. We must look at all aspects of the dream to determine its meaning. Perhaps it was a wishful dream for this type of relationship and she still sought a soul mate.

The dream could have been symbolic of a future husband or a strongly held desire, if it did not fit the reality of her current relationship. Remember, dreams are messages from the soul.

Another perspective of flying dreams is that they can reflect a need to be more grounded. This means: "having your feet firmly planted on the ground" in your waking life. After a flying dream, ask yourself if you need to be more grounded in your personal or working life.

Sometimes in a flying dream, the dreamer is only able to achieve a limited elevation or fly for a limited period of time. For example, a dreamer may find herself barely able to rise above power lines, as she takes flight.

Some interpretations for dreams of this type include the following:

- Power lines may symbolize control, an electrical charge, communication, empowerment and obstacles.

- Power lines may represent the dreamer's personal power. They can also symbolize an attempt to connect with a higher power.

- Trying to rise above some kind of limitation.

- A need to change direction.

    A need to deal with control issues.

    A communication problem that is restricting the dreamer in her waking life.

Flight Details

Pretend that you are an air traffic controller in an observation tower. Let's take a look at some details of your "flight":

    Flying a steady course and maintaining altitude could indicate that your life is on course and going well.

    It could also indicate that you will achieve your goals and aspirations without too much difficulty.

    Struggling to reach the right altitude could mean that you are off course or reaching for something for which you are not yet ready.

    It could also signify a need to change your goals and "flight" plans.

    A sudden storm, while you are flying, could suggest that you will soon encounter a challenge or obstacle.

Flying dreams are, for most people, expressions of empowerment and perhaps a need to be free. Flying dreams allow you to reach heights (goals) that you may never have dreamed possible in your waking life. Those dreams may be telling you to set loftier goals.

> A dream of trying to fly away from attackers can demonstrate personal empowerment. Taking control and trying to escape, indicates that you don't want to be a victim.
>
> Should the pursuers catch you before you are airborne, you may conclude that there is something that you must face, in your waking life, before you can "take off" in a new direction.

Dreaming of objects in your path may reflect waking life obstacles, which need to be to overcome. Some examples follow:

- Buildings: May symbolize obstacles, or people who could be holding you back.

- Trees: Any type of tree can indicate that personal growth is required.

Small trees can represent new relationships and personal growth.

Tall, bushy trees can symbolize high intellect, tall people and those who have reached great achievements ("great heights").

A tree with a lot of branches could symbolize a person with a lot of connections.

Fruit trees can represent creativity, health, beauty and new ideas ("bearing new fruit").

Dreams of soaring freely, without hindrance, are powerful indicators of: confidence, strength, freedom, happiness, feeling of being empowered, being in control or being "on top of the world".

Floating Dreams

Have you ever, in a dream, floated on a cloud and felt wonderfully free? What was it like? Were you floating above your bed? Or, were you floating over a city or the countryside?

Floating dreams are often dreams of freedom or happiness. Sometimes they symbolize drifting, without any goals. You can float until you find an answer or solution to a problem. Or, you can float until you gain a different perspective on a particular situation.

Floating is a wonderful state of relaxation. In such a state you can let things come and go. You can take all the time you want to explore and enjoy your life.

Perhaps you have obtained a goal and you would like to savor the feelings and not worry about the next stage of your life. Floating dreams allow you do just that.

Sometimes floating dreams can point out negative aspects in your life. This could be an inability to find a direction or to take control of your life.

You could be avoiding making some decision; you find it easier to just drift and be free from stress. Floating in a dream could be saying: "I'll think about it". Floating could also indicate that you are having an out-of-body experience (astral travel).

I would like to share one of my floating dreams; it was wonderful and powerful. Then, Karin, Rod and I will analyze.

> *I was lying on a blanket under a tree. It was a starlit*
> *night.*
>
> *I felt the blanket slowly lift off the ground; I was floating up to the stars. I found myself looking down on the whole planet and at the whole galaxy. Everything was gentle and serene. I wasn't a bit afraid.*
>
> *I saw a brilliant star coming towards me. I gently merged with its energy and light. I felt as if I had become one with the universe. It was wonderful, timeless feeling. I felt a great peace and contentment.*
>
> *When I felt totally blissful and connected to everything, I floated back to earth and to the blanket below the tree.*
>
> *It was a mystical, magical and powerful dream.*

Rod: Wow! What a wonderful dream. The universe was the largest thing in the dream. That means that you were the universe.

Karin: You cannot get any larger than the universe!

Rod: Irene, what life process were you going through at the time? (**Key #7: The action in the dream describes the process you are living through.**) Were you asking for insight into your career?

Irene: That's a good question. Had something in my waking life triggered the dream? Or, had I been asking my guides for assistance on something of importance?

At the time, I was questioning my life's purpose. The dream made me feel totally connected to all things. I emerged from the dream knowing that I was on the right path. I was "floating on cloud nine" for weeks after the dream.

Since that dream, I have consistently felt connected to my purpose in life. The dream was a priceless gift. It confirmed, in a very personal and powerful way, that I (and everyone else) was connected to something much greater than myself. It also confirmed that the universe, with all its magic and wisdom, is available to me and to all those who seek it.

There is an expression (I do not know the author) that says: "let go and let God". I fully understood that after the dream. The dream reaffirmed my spiritual path. I felt connected to everything and was closer to bliss than I had ever been!

Karin: We do not normally experience pure bliss and harmony in our waking lives. But, we can experience those things in the dream state.

Irene: I think I may have also experienced what happens at death—a very gentle return to a natural state of being, a return to "home" and the universe.

Floating can often signify an escape from reality. It can indicate avoidance, denial and indecision about something in your life. It can also signal a need to be more grounded in your waking life.

Falling, flying and floating dreams often relate to simply experiencing yourself in a non-physical or spiritual form.

> Too many dreams with the same theme can be a "wake up call".
>
> This includes dreams of falling, flying and floating.

Part 6: Relationships

Love Relationships

How many times have you had dreams filled with desires, romance, a mysterious rendezvous, a wedding or a long awaited fulfillment?

Those dreams are usually based on your desires or the relationships you have with others in your waking life. They can also reflect the relationship that you have with yourself.

You may agonize over your relationships, especially those that are unsatisfactory in some way. Dreams allow you to gain a different perspective on them. Dreams can help you to understand any problems and identify what you really want from your relationships.

In the dream state, your emotions are much more profound than those in your waking life. For that reason, dream messages go beyond love, hate, guilt, fear, loyalty, etc.

Dreams can teach you to deal with your reality. Interpreting your dreams can sometimes be uncomfortable. The associated emotions could be raw and demanding. It is quite probable that those are the same feelings that you have pushed away in your waking life.

Whether it is a nightmare, a dream filled with passion, romance or infatuation, dreams can show you the things that you need to see, feel, change, create or understand.

Imagine that you were in a loving relationship and that you had a dream about a wedding. You could readily conclude that the dream was symbolic of some form of union. Now, analyze the role that you played in the dream; that role would be significant.

Pretend that the dream scenario had you as a member of the wedding party or as a guest, rather than as the bride.

The dream may have left you confused. If you had been the bride, the dream could have confirmed your desire to commit to a marriage. It could have also assured you that your man was the right one for you. But, you were not the bride.

You must ask yourself why you placed yourself in a role other than as the bride. Your higher self could be telling you to look at something in your waking relationship.

Perhaps you or your partner could have a commitment issue. Could you be sensing, but not acknowledging that in your waking life? If so, the dream could be telling you that. The dream could also be telling you that your waking life partner is not the one for you to marry.

When analyzing relationship dreams, please consider the following:

- Your emotional state in the dream. Ponder what it could mean.

- Whether a dream wedding was joyful or uncomfortable.

- If you were happy in the role of a guest or as a wedding party member. And, if so, why?

- If you need reaffirmation of your partner's love and commitment.

- If there could be rivalry, or some other issue, that you are not consciously aware of in your waking life relationship.

- If your sub-conscious was telling you that your waking relationship needed to change.

I have frequently been asked the following question: "is it possible to make a love connection with another soul in a dream?" The answer is yes! If you can make spiritual connections with guides and loved  ones, in dreams, you can also make loving connections to other souls (people).

I would like to share the dreams of two of my clients. Both illustrate the power of thoughts and of dreams; both illustrate the "Law of Attraction". A common thread in both dreams is a strong, focused desire.

The first case is that of a young woman who longed for a meaningful love relationship. She received seemingly confusing messages from her dreams and intuition. This is her story:

I had recently broken off with a man whose initials *were TJ and who drove a red truck.*

After the breakup, I began to consciously and frequently affirm that I was very deserving of a committed, loving relationship.

I began having dreams about a red truck in my driveway; I knew that it belonged to a man who would play a significant role in my life. At the same time, I began "seeing" the initials TJ in my mind's eye. I knew that this was an important sign.

I was confused; I knew that I didn't love my previous boyfriend. Was the universe telling me to reconcile with him? I wasn't sure what to do.

The dreams and visions went on for a few months; I knew that they were important messages from my subconscious and the universe. I struggled to have faith that their meanings would be revealed at the right time.

Then, unexpectedly I met another man; he too bore the initials TJ, but he didn't drive a red truck. I didn't think a lot about him because I knew that the red truck was such an important omen.

One day, TJ (the second man) called me to say that he was stranded on the highway and needed to get to a nearby city that afternoon. I told him that I would pick him up and drive him to that city. When I dropped him off, I invited him to come to my place that evening for dinner.

When he arrived, he was driving a red truck! He had purchased it earlier that day, in the adjacent city. At that moment I knew, without a shadow of a doubt, that he was the man for me. I sobbed in gratitude, wonder and joy. I had met my soul mate!

A happy post-script to this story is that my client and TJ have been together, happily, since that day.

My second client also wanted a special love relationship and she had very specific terms for it. She lived a demanding life, with little free time and had no desire to marry. Nevertheless, she wanted companionship. She wanted a man, but she also wanted to be free to travel, enjoy her friends and to pursue her many interests.

She knew that her attitude was selfish and perhaps idealistic. That did not stop her from longing for the perfect man to fit her lifestyle. She constantly affirmed her intention. One night she had the following dream:

I was going on a holiday. I was at a train station waiting to board.

Another train nearby was unloading passengers. I watched a tall, handsome man get off that train.

I saw my perfect man! He was everything that I had imagined. I wondered if he lived in the city.

The dream seemed to take place in another time, yet it was so real.

The memory of the dream lingered for days; she fantasized about the man from the train. They were the perfect couple! She saw them traveling together and having fun. At the same time, she retained the freedom that she cherished.

She daydreamed that he shared her perspective on companionship and freedom. She placed herself in the role that she desired; she was so happy.

She called and asked me to interpret her dream. My intuitive impression was that she was "on track". Her dream was telling her that her wish would come true. Three months later she met her dream man in a railway car section at a restaurant called *The Sidetrack Café*.

This couple has an unusual relationship; but it seems to suit them to perfection. They are committed to each other, yet they both pursue individual interests and friends. They have been together for more than five years. They must be "on the right track!"

Dreams about Parents & Sibling.

If you reflected on all of your relationships, the ones involving your parents and siblings would likely be the most important and most memorable.

Parents are your first role models; they are your teachers, protectors and authority figures. They help you to develop your interpersonal communication skills, as well as a broad range of other social, mental, emotional and physical abilities.

Childhood is a time of growth, play and rapid learning. It is a time in which you learn about power, security, loyalty, support, unconditional love and a multitude of other things. All of these things are generally experienced through your parents and siblings.

Usually, significant love and other emotions are found in family relationships. Thus, it is not surprising when family members play significant roles in your dreams.

Dreams about your parents generally deal with the issue of love and reflect what each parent means to you. In your dreams, each parent generally assumes specific roles just as they do in your waking life. For example, one parent could represent authority, strength and support. The other could typify playfulness, affection, gentleness and nurturing.

If you dreamed about your parents, when you were a child, you would see them in a specific way; for example, teachers or protectors. Then, if you dreamt about them when you were an adult, you would also view them in a different way. As an adult, you might dream of them as friends or colleagues.

When analyzing dreams that involve your parents or siblings (as well as other relationships), it is important that you identify your feelings about those people. That will help you to interpret the dream's message.

If affection and support are lacking in your adult waking relationships, dreams about your parents could reflect your need for nurturing or companionship. Dreams about the love and support that you received from your parents could mean that you need to nurture yourself. They could also mean that you need to be more self-reliant.

A child being raised in a single parent home could have dreams in which the missing parent appears. The child is simply creating a fantasy parent to give her what she longs for in her waking life.

I had dreams of this sort for a period of time after my mother left my dad; I was about 10 years old at the time. I dreamed that I was my father. In the dreams, I was loving and kind to my mother; I had taken on the role of "husband".

The dreams were very confusing to me. My mother explained that I was transferring myself into my father's role. In that role, I was attempting to win her back. She also explained that I likely created a father, in my dreams, to replace the one who was missing in my waking life.

Later in life, when I reflected on those dreams, I wondered if they meant that I had taken over my father's role, in my waking life, and had become the "man of the family". In many ways, I played that role until I was 17 years old. I did my best to take care of my mother during those years, frequently assuming responsibilities that were beyond my years.

Dreams are vehicles to express all kinds of emotions. A child who is being raised in an abusive home could act out feelings of aggression, fear or powerlessness in his dreams. He might even dream that his abuser died. Such a dream would reflect a clear desire to escape the cruelty. That same child could create a loving, fantasy parent in a dream, in the same way that a child of a single parent would.

It is important to remember that dreams fulfill fantasies and are forms of escape. It doesn't matter if they are pretty, nice, awful, wicked or bad. They are forms of emotional release and thus are healing.

It is also important to remember that a regular occurrence of these types of dreams could signal the need for professional assistance. Professional therapy could treat the cause of the dreams and avert other unwanted emotions, such as fear and guilt, for dreaming the dreams.

Several of my adult clients have dreamed that one or both of their parents had died. Naturally, they were deeply disturbed by the dreams.

Dreams like that are not uncommon, nor are the dreamers' reactions uncommon. Such dreams do not necessarily mean that a parent's death is imminent. You must remember that dreams speak to you in symbols. Your challenge is to interpret the symbols, so that you can understand the dream's message.

Consider the following when analyzing a dream of a parent's death:

- A relationship change, in your waking life, with either or both parents could have taken place. For example, an old hurt or other issue could have "died" and been "laid to rest".

- You may have been trying to "bury" some unresolved conflict.

- A change in your parents' relationship may have occurred. This could have been a divorce or separation; something between them could have "died".

- Any change in their accommodations. Perhaps they moved from the family home into a retirement complex.

- A role reversal may have occurred or is underway. This commonly happens when parents grow older and their adult children become their caregivers.

Lying to parents, siblings or others in dreams may be symbolic of your keeping something from them. Such dreams could also reflect a lack of trust or perhaps self-deception.

Being abandoned by parents, in your dreams, could be linked to feelings of insecurity in your waking life. Abandonment feelings could also be related to financial woes. They could also reflect concerns about the people in your life who offer you guidance, security and support.

Sometimes, your dreams can reflect exactly how you feel about your parents or others in your life. That is, they can be interpreted literally, with little need to analyze the symbols.

The following dream, from one of my clients, illustrates maternal love and support. His dream could be interpreted literally.

I was sitting in the backyard, crying my eyes out. I was about six years old. I was not physically hurt but I was emotionally upset.

I felt lost and frightened. All of a sudden my mother appeared. She bent down and picked me up.

Instantly, I stopped crying; I felt safe, loved and protected.

If your children are experiencing troubling dreams, try to determine if they are feeling upset or insecure about something. Their dreams can reveal a wealth of information about their waking concerns.

If you have dreams about yourself as a child, those dreams could reflect a desire for the carefree days of childhood. Dreams of being a child again could also indicate a need to lighten up and have more fun. Alternately, they could be telling you that you are too dependent on your parents or significant others in your life. It may be time to break free from parental ties.

Sometimes, parents' dreams about their children can be anxiety-filled. This is particularly true for first time parents. New parents have shared, with me, frightening dreams about their children. They dreamed of losing their children in a crowd, forgetting them at a store, accidentally smothering them, etc. Those dreams reflected their anxieties that they would unintentionally hurt or neglect their children.

No doubt you want to be the perfect parent and to give your children the best guidance and care. Anxiety dreams can make you feel incompetent and imperfect. Do not let such dreams upset you. Accept the fact that all parents have anxieties about their children. Your anxiety dreams will no doubt decrease as your parental experience increases.

Sometimes parents' dreams about their children can be literal, rather than symbolic. Literal dreams seem to be very detailed and specific in nature. That is because parents, especially mothers, can be very psychically attuned to their children.

One of my clients came to me for advice because she had dreamed that two of her children had been in accidents. The first involved a bicycle, the second a skateboard.

I recommended that she review the rules of safety with each of her children, because the dreams would likely occur (because of the graphic nature of details). The accidents did happen, but they were less severe than they could have been, probably because of her warnings.

Wanting and Manifesting a Relationship

Can you meet someone in a dream, before you do so in your waking life? Absolutely! You can find, encourage and improve relationships through your dreams.

Several of my clients had longed to find their soul mates. Many saw them in their dreams, before they met them in their waking lives. Some clients wanted to find new bosses or business partners; others wanted to meet their future children. Most were able to do so, in their dreams.

Can you first meet someone in a dream?

If you are seeking a special relationship, visualize what that person or relationship would be like. Keep that intention strong; then, before you go to sleep ask for a dream about that person.

This may take several attempts before you see results. Please do not give up. Eventually, you will dream about that special someone.

In a similar way, you can use your dreams to send love vibrations to someone you know and want to attract on a romantic basis. Send him loving thoughts during the day. Then, just before you drift off to sleep, ask to have him come into your dreams. When he appears, ask him to phone you!

This is a very powerful technique; please take care to use it ethically and responsibly. Ensure that you send the dream vibrations only to those people who are unattached and available for romance.

You can use your dreams to improve existing relationships. For example, you may want to tell a partner or friend something to resolve a misunderstanding. Set the intention, of what you desire, before going to sleep. Then allow a dream to give you messages and insights on what you must do to improve the relationship.

Be patient when asking for help from your dreams and thoroughly analyze each one to uncover its message. Hidden thoughts, feelings and desires may be found in your dreams.

Consider sharing your dreams with your mate. This practice could open new channels of communication and subsequently enhance intimacy. You may discover things about yourself or each other, that you never before considered.

Your dreams may offer you considerable insight about your relationships. Merely set the intention that you will find wisdom in your dreams. Then, be open to receiving it. Trust the messages that you receive; they will never steer you wrong.

Messages from your dreams can be hidden in unexpected symbols. For example:

1. Money.

- May indicate feelings of enslavement, either financially or emotionally to someone or something in your life.
- May symbolize giving or receiving in relationships, especially on the emotional plane.
- May depict generosity or greed, when one partner has more than the other.
- May reflect insecurities, extravagance or indulgence of one partner, when the other entered the relationship with debts or is irresponsible with money.
- Saving, investing or financial planning can reflect fears, for example, a lack of funds or poverty.
- Dropping or losing money can reflect insecurities; for example, loss of a relationship or emotional insecurity.
- Receiving money is generally a good omen; it often indicates that abundance (financial and emotional) is coming into your life.

2. A Ticking Clock.

- Clocks always symbolize time in some form, for example: the passing of time, an age reference or a sense of urgency.

- May suggest that something important or ominous will happen in a relationship. It may be time for it to end.

- May indicate the exact time that you will meet a special person. The time could also depict additional information, such as a favorite number or preferred time of day.

- Could mean that a woman's "biological clock is ticking" and that it is time to have a child.

- Could indicate, for both men and women, that time is passing too quickly, particularly if they haven't found their perfect mates or achieved long held goals.

- Alarm clocks or slow, "bonging" sounds could be warnings of danger.

- Arriving early/ahead of schedule could indicate eagerness or waiting for something to happen or someone to appear.

- Lateness could indicate the value given or not given to a situation or person. It could signify a lack of respect or attention to someone or something.

- A clock going in reverse could indicate a need to review or accept something from your past. It could also indicate that the dream is taking you back in time, to a previous life.

- Being a clock-watcher could reflect a concern that life is passing you by or that you are wasting your time. It could also represent pressure to accomplish something or fulfill an obligation within a specific period of time.

Animals in Dreams

Pets

Pets that have died can appear in your dreams. They can send you messages, just as deceased family members and friends can. They can offer comfort by letting you know that they are safe and spiritually close to you. Their messages are usually based on their personalities.

Sometimes, pets in dreams can symbolize qualities that you need to develop; they often symbolize love and caring. Or, they can represent something about yourself that needs to be recognized and understood. Look at the characteristics of the animal for clues.

A baby animal could be symbolic of you as a child. It could be showing you that you need to nurture your "inner child". Or, it could be telling you that you need to be gentle with someone in your life who is vulnerable.

Any animal can carry a message. A young animal with its mother could symbolize family, nurturing, support, vulnerability and protection.

The type of animal and its condition can convey a wealth of information. More specific information follows:

Wounded Animals

A hurt or wounded animal can be symbolic of painful waking life events, both recent and in the far past. Wounds from childhood or a past life event can be represented in an animal dream. Wounded animals can symbolize a wounded body or spirit.

Look at the characteristics of the dream animal to gain further information. For example, if the animal is caught in a trap, ask yourself if you are feeling trapped, in some part of your waking life. If the animal has a wounded leg, it could indicate that the pain of moving forward is keeping you stuck in a rut. Trapped animals are not uncommon in dreams.

Dreams of wounded animals could symbolize that you were "licking your wounds" or feeling helpless about some waking life incident. A hurt puppy could indicate that you felt hurt by something or someone in your waking life.

Scary animals

A deformity in an animal could relate to a deformity, fear, injury or poor self-image that you could be experiencing in your waking life.

A pet with a missing limb could symbolize that your life is "out of balance" in some way. Or, that you are "limping along" in life. It could also represent feelings of worthlessness, inadequacy or incompetence.

If a dream animal, with a deformity, is otherwise particularly attractive, it could reflect a belief that you have some kind of major flaw. You might feel that this flaw detracts from your beauty, both in body and character.

One of my clients had a dog with only one eye; its right eye had been lost in an accident. She doted on her dog, like it was her child. After a time, she began having trouble with her right eye.

One night she dreamed that her dog lost its other eye. She became extremely concerned about how helpless her dog would be if it were totally blind.

I tried to help her to understand that she was too closely identifying with the dog's plight. The problems that she was experiencing with her right eye were in sympathy for the dog's blindness. I helped her to grasp the idea that her obsession with her dog wasn't allowing her to "see" how it was negatively affecting her life.

I suggested that she seek professional counseling to better understand her relationship with her dog. Also, to explore potential feelings of helplessness that she might have been experiencing. She took my advice. She later told me that when she understood the connection between her eye trouble and the dog's blindness, her eye improved.

Scary Animals

Animals that repulse or frighten you, can symbolize your (or others) shadow side. Scary animals are often cold-blooded, like reptiles and snakes. They may symbolize that the dreamer is "cold-blooded" in her waking life. Or, that she wishes she could be more detached, unemotional or "cold" about a specific situation or person.

Scary animals can also portray hostility, betrayal and death. What they mean depends on the interpretation of the dreamer.

Mystical Animals

It is possible for you to dream that you are a unicorn or centaur (a being that is half animal and half human). This could suggest that you will experience something magical. Or, it could symbolize that a transformation of some kind will occur. Unicorns are often symbolic of playfulness and innocence.

Prehistoric Animals

Prehistoric animals can represent a previous lifetime memory. They can also represent some old issue or memory that you could be digging up. It could signify that it is time to resolve that issue.

Totem Animals

Many aboriginal cultures believe that each person is born with one or more totem (spirit) animals. Some cultures believe that each person walks the earth with seven to nine spirit animals. Regardless, each totem animal endows its human with special talents, medicine, protection and magic.

Shamans believe that an animal chooses a human and not the reverse. The reason is because the individual could choose unwisely. For example, a person could select a glamorous or powerful animal, such as a wolf or eagle, rather than one that was harmonious to his character.

Should you have a dream about an animal, you must ask yourself what that animal means to you. A fox could signify craftiness, a horse could represent power and a dog could mean loyalty.

The dream could indicate that you are beginning to recognize some of that animal's characteristics within yourself. Or, it could suggest that you need to apply those traits to your present day waking life.

If you want to learn more about animals and their gifts, please research Ted Andrews' work. He is one of the leading authorities on this subject. One of his books is *Animal Speak*.

A Word of Caution

Just like everything else in dreams, an animal can be a part of yourself. Further, parts of the animal, such as the eyes, can represent your eyes.

Never harm, maim or kill an animal in a dream, whether at the time that it occurs or when going back into it. The same holds true for humans who try to harm you. Harming or killing an animal or human is akin to damaging or killing a part of yourself.

Rather than killing or harming living beings, in your dreams, let them be messengers. Examine their characteristics and actions and interpret the message as best as you can.

Erotic Dreams

Almost everyone has experienced sexual or erotic dreams at one time or another. Such dreams can occur when your sexuality first awakens. Some people experience these types of dreams all of their lives.

Erotic dreams can be emotionally upsetting. Upon awakening, you may feel guilt or shame. Try to let go of those negative responses. Rather, try to understand that the dream was sending you a message. Try to decode that message. Erotic dreams can carry messages about your emotions, mind and spirit, as well as your body.

One of my male clients had the following dream:

> *I was in a house with many other people. I went down to the basement and found myself swimming under an ocean. I swam up to some reeds.*
>
> *Through the reeds, I saw a naked man making love to a woman.*
>
> *Swimming nearby were three large, green, toothy alligators. I wondered why the man was not worried when they were so close to danger.*
>
> *Suddenly I found myself naked, making love to a woman; we were deep under water. We made love for what seemed like many minutes. We decided to go upstairs to continue making love.*
>
> *When I awoke, I felt no regret or guilt, only elation.*

Karin: At first, the dreamer seemed to be in a passive state, observing others in an intimate act.

Irene: The dreamer could have been lacking physical intimacy in his life. Swimming in water is symbolic of something deeply emotional. Being naked in water depicts great emotional vulnerability, as well as sensuality.

Rod: Swimming naked in the reeds seemed to be very sensual. The acts of love seemed suggestive of hidden desires for sexual fulfillment.

Karin: The proximity of the alligators seemed to say that the dreamer felt it was dangerous to have sexual desires.

Irene: The three alligators could represent three fears: fear of getting hurt, fear of hurting others, or fear of repercussions due to his sexual desires. Perhaps the alligators were a warning.

Going upstairs, in the house, could have symbolized bringing those desires out into the open. The second floor of the house can represent the future. Perhaps the dreamer was going to experience fulfillment of his desires in the near future.

Karin: From a non-sexual perspective, the dreamer connected with a woman. That could represent a way to reconnect to his softer, creative side. Both he and the woman rose from deep water to above the surface. The dreamer's creativity could be emerging.

Rod: The deep water could represent something buried in the past, something that was coming to the surface.

Irene: An erotic dream isn't always what it seems to be at first glance. The dream is always about the dreamer. It is exploring the messages from the sub-conscious mind.

Look at your dreams in many different ways. **(Key #10: Be willing to look at a dream from multiple perspectives, when analyzing it.)**

Consider the mental, emotional, physical and spiritual aspects. Allow your imagination to take you beyond the boundaries of your usual thinking. Accept all interpretations as valid.

> Erotic dreams hold powerful emotions.

One client shared her dreams of having many lovers. Those dreams created great stress in her waking life because she loved her husband very much. I asked if their relationship was lacking in intimacy; she confessed that it was. The dreams could have been an expression of her desire for emotional, sexual or physical intimacy.

Many teenagers have shared their sex dreams with me. Often times, those dreams caused the teens to have orgasms in their sleep. They would wake up feeling guilty, ashamed or confused. Erotic dreams need not elicit such negative emotions; they are normal experiences.

Adults have also shared, with me, their erotic dreams. Some of those had the (married) dreamer with another man or woman. The same guilt, confusion and shame were experienced. This is so unnecessary.

It is easy to be distracted by the sheer power of the imagery and settings in erotic dreams. Try not to let that happen. You need to determine how the action, in those dreams, could be related to your waking life.

As a result of my workshops and private consultations, I have observed something interesting about the incidence of erotic and fantasy dreams. Heavy-set people seem to have more of these than slimmer people do.

I think that these dreams could be an expression of low esteem, poor self-confidence and insufficient intimacy in their waking lives.

Violence in Dreams

Some clients have shared their dreams of violence. In those dreams, they had committed murder, robberies and other crimes against society. They awoke with intense feelings of guilt and shame; often those feelings were carried for years.

> No dream should make you feel guilty.
> Never punish yourself for its contents.

Violence in dreams usually indicates suppressed emotions, such as anger, hate and rage. Those emotions can be directed toward yourself or others.

Murdering someone in a dream could be symbolic of "killing off" some part of yourself that you don't like. As I indicated, in the section on animals, killing someone is not a wise thing to do because it represents killing some part of yourself.

I have never known anyone who has experienced his own murder in a dream. I would interpret such an event as a release of something significant in his waking life. Such a death could be symbolic of a rebirth.

> Most dreams are symbolic.
> They should not be interpreted literally.

Subconscious fears, from every stage of your life, can emerge in your dreams. Think of those dreams as ceremonial; they are simply a way of opening, then closing doors to unwanted emotions from your past. They may be healing acts.

Dreams provide a safe avenue to explore and express unwanted feelings. Never judge your dreams or the dreams of others. Dreams are emotional releases; they are not sins.

Taboos in Dreams

By now you can see that you may not always have "nice" dreams. Socially taboo subjects can appear in dreams. These can include such things as burning a cross or a flag, sodomy, or homosexual acts in a heterosexual's dream.

Dreams with taboo subjects do not mean that you are a depraved person. A dream in which you were sodomized could mean that you were feeling vulnerable, abused or exposed in your waking life. It could also mean that you "felt like an ass" or were "em—bare—assed" about something.

Similarly, a heterosexual's dream about homosexual acts could reflect the dreamer's curiosity about the homosexual life style and intimate expressions of love.

An unrelated, but also potentially uncomfortable dream subject is religion. Sometimes disgusting or seemingly disrespectful scenes can occur in dreams with a religious theme.

For example, a person could dream of raping a nun and subsequently feel extreme shame. The dream could be symbolic of taking something by force that was off limits in the dreamer's waking life.

Another person could dream that she had a conversation with the Buddha. This could make her feel that she was being disloyal to the beliefs of her Christian church.

Dreams with taboo subjects are permissible in the dream environment. In dreams, there are no rules or boundaries; earthly logic can't be applied. So, please don't dismiss taboo dreams; they may hold valuable information.

On the other hand, sometimes you must just look at a dream and let it go. That is; don't obsess over its meaning and don't let it upset you.

Dream Normalcy

What is normal in the world of dreams? Everything! This includes fantasy, realism, forecasts, fears and plain old silliness! Each dream has relevance and needs to be accepted and explored.

Dreams hold concepts, illusions, insights, tools, frustrations and influences from people and events in your life. These things are constantly evolving, both in your dream and waking worlds.

Dreams are part of your personal growth. They can help you to discover the shadow side of yourself. This, in turn, encourages self-understanding and self-acceptance.

Remember **Key #10: Be willing to look at a dream from multiple perspectives, when analyzing it.** Think outside the box!

Part 7: Other Spiritual Dimensions

Requesting Guidance from Dreams

Have you ever wished that you had answers to the following questions?

- Will I get a raise this year?
- How should I handle that situation at work?
- Will I pass my exams?
- When will I meet my soul mate?
- How can I identify guides in my dreams?

Guidance for managing difficult or perplexing situations can often be found in your dreams. Similarly, answers to important questions can be accessed through the dream state.

When I was a child, I was taught to look for guidance from my spirit guides and loved ones who had died. That guidance was often found in my dreams.

Requesting guidance through dreams is easy to do. Simply ask that you receive direction or answers to your questions in your dreams. The timing, setting and phrasing of your questions are important. Be aware, that decoding the answers and guidance can sometimes be difficult.

> If you want to ask questions to be answered in your dreams, do not watch TV or read before going to bed.

As previously indicated, what you see and hear before going to sleep can become part of your dream life. Asking a question, to be answered in a dream, during a TV commercial, while leafing through a magazine or following a spat with your partner is not apt to work. The answer could be tainted by the mental images and emotional debris from those activities; thus it may not be accurate.

Try the following method; I have had good success with it. Begin the process early in the day. Focus on the issue that you would like guidance on or the question that you would like answered. This sets the intention that you will receive the information through your dreams.

From time to time during the day, think about the situation or ask the question. At bedtime ask your guides, your higher self or the angels to provide an answer or guidance in your dreams. This reinforces your intention that your dreams will send you the information that you desire. Then, allow yourself to drift into sleep, fully expecting that you will receive the information that you are seeking.

If you do not get the information the first night, repeat the process for the next day or two. Answers don't always come immediately or clearly. Take note of anything that you do receive; the symbols or words may be the start of the answer.

Repeat your request for at least three consecutive nights; ask for clarity each time. Record each dream; this will help you to understand the dream's message.

To illustrate the effectiveness of this, I will share one of my experiences with this process. A few years ago, I wanted to meet someone to help me with marketing ideas and solutions for some products that I wanted to sell. I asked my dreams to show me the person who would help me.

In the first dream, I was driving my car. Someone I didn't know handed me a map. It was too cloudy to read it; I wished that there had been better light. When I woke up, I decided that the map was from one of my guides, but I wasn't sure what it meant. I didn't know what to do. I wondered if the clouds meant that my question had been too vague.

That evening, I repeated my request with greater focus. I then asked to receive clarity on the first dream. I dreamed that I was in a shopping mall. The mall was having a huge sale; each store had bargain tables set up in front of its entrance. I found myself walking in the mall; I stopped in front of a travel agency that was giving away free maps of Edmonton.

I awoke the next morning and thought about the dream. I wondered if I needed to go to a mall. That evening, a flyer appeared in the local newspaper; it advertised a sidewalk sale in a nearby mall. I knew that I had to go to the mall during the sale.

On the third evening, I repeated my request in the same way that I had done the previous night. I dreamt that I was introduced to a woman I didn't know, by another woman I didn't know. The first woman told me that I was lucky that I had dropped in on a Saturday; she added that she was about to go to lunch. The second woman had long, red hair and was wearing a beige suit. She seemed excited to meet me.

I woke up knowing that I had to go to the mall before noon on the Saturday of the sale; I also knew that I had to go at noon. Just before noon, I walked up to a sales table that was located in front of a travel agency. I began chatting to the  sales lady about what I did and about my desire to sell certain products.

By now you have probably guessed what happened next. A woman, with long red hair, wearing a beige suit approached us. She was a friend of the travel agent. We were introduced; she was the person I had been seeking! She helped me launch my products.

My dreams provided the guidance that I had requested. I encourage you to use your dreams to help you. Don't give up if you don't immediately receive the answers that you want. Persevere; your persistence will be rewarded.

Steps for Requesting Guidance From Your Dreams

"Let me sleep on it" is a familiar expression; it holds great meaning. Many people go to sleep with an unresolved situation or problem on their minds. Often, they wake up with a solution without understanding that it came to them in their dreams.

If you would like to learn how to ask for and receive answers in your dreams, try the following method:

- An hour before bed, place some note paper and a pen on your night table. If these items are already there, pick them up and put them back down. This action affirms the seriousness of your intention.

- Mentally, review the question or situation for which you would like assistance. Affirm that an answer or enlightenment will come, as a result of your asking. This also affirms the intention of your quest.

- As illustrated earlier, it often takes three consecutive nights of asking in order to gain complete information. Sometimes the information/answer comes in pieces, over the course of these nights. You can ask for clarity on the second and third nights.

- Keep in mind that the answer to your question could come in the form of symbolism and that symbolism could be quite bizarre. Alternately, the answer or guidance could be very straightforward and easy to interpret.

I don't know why this ritual works, but it does. Perhaps, some part of your subconscious mind accepts your direction. Then, it solves the problem or finds the answer to your question.

Dream of finding your one true love!

Set the intention and be patient.
Be open to the symbolism and your interpretation.

Here is another dream that illustrates how a client received an answer to her question, over a three-day period. She used the aforementioned method for getting answers from dreams.

She went to bed with a strong desire and trust that she would receive an answer.

*The first morning that she woke, after asking her question, she could only recall the color baby **blue**.*

*She repeated her question the second night. The next morning all she remembered was the number **twelve**.*

*Patiently and persistently, she asked the same question on the third night. During a dream, she saw a calendar showing the month of **April**.*

She had the answer to her question, which had been "when will I have my first grandchild?"

Her grandson was born on April 12 in the following year!

Dreams and Self Growth

Dreams can help you to uncover hidden parts of yourself. They can also help you to understand your unconscious needs and desires. Dreams access information not only from your subconscious, but also from the spiritual realm.

If you are open-minded and ready to let your dreams guide you, they will. They can prompt you to make decisions that can change your life. This is no exaggeration.

Finding Answers in Dreams

If you are interested in exploring the reasons for your existence or understanding the motivation for your behavior, try asking your dream self for insight.

Ask only one question at a time. If you ask more than one, it will only confuse the issue and make the answers difficult to decode.

Ask your question during the quiet time that occurs just before sleep. That question could be one of the following:

- Who am I? Am I on the right path for my spiritual growth?
- What is my purpose?
- Should I change my career?
- Who are my guides?
- How many children will I have?
- Will I live a long and happy life?
- What are my intentions?
- Am I ready to work with my guides and angels?
- Am I ready to reach my goals?

> Do not ask more than one question at a time. It will only confuse the issue. Then, the answers are apt to be inaccurate.

When you wake up, you may have only a partial answer. As previously indicated, it often takes three or more consecutive nights to receive a complete answer to your question. Please do not give up. Repeat the question each night, until you are satisfied.

Dream answers come in the form of symbols, metaphors and emotions. Sometimes the answers come in a sequence that unfolds like a movie or a book.

Answers from Guides

Try the following exercise to solicit answers from departed loved ones or your guides. This technique has worked for many of my clients.

- Find two small pieces of paper. On one piece print the letter "Y" for yes, on the other print "N" for no.

- Place the papers side by side, about two inches apart, on your dresser or someplace where they won't be disturbed. It makes no difference whether they are face up or face down. Make sure that there are no air currents that could move them.

- Place an unwrapped and rounded toothpick in a vertical position midway between the papers. (Note: The flat toothpicks do not roll too well for this exercise.)

- Before going to bed, ask a question that can be answered with a yes or no. Then, ask the universe to give you the answer by moving the toothpick in the correct direction.

- The answer will be the one that the toothpick rolls to or clearly points to.

- What if the toothpick assumes a horizontal position or doesn't move at all?

First, the question may not have been asked with sufficient clarity. Next, it could indicate that either option would be fine. Third, it could mean that the situation was too complex for a yes/no answer, in spite of the question that asked for a yes or a no response. Finally, it could mean that the answer was "maybe".

Remember, you are trying to connect to another dimension and it could take several nights to get an answer.

Dreaming for Other People

One of the most amazing dream experiences that I ever had concerned my husband. In the dream, he was at work sitting at his desk. I heard him talking to the people who were around him. The discussion seemed to be of great interest to everyone; it was causing a great deal of anxiety.

The dream seemed very real; it was rich in detail. Because of the tension in the dream, I had a very restless night.

In the morning I told my husband about the dream. He was stunned. He told me that the dream reflected exactly what had occurred the day before, just prior to the end of the workday. He revealed that he had been anxious and concerned about the issue, just like everyone else.

He had been preoccupied about it prior to falling asleep. He had anticipated a sleepless night due to this situation, but confessed that he had slept like a baby. (Of course he did, I processed it for him!)

I was shocked, but thrilled to discover that I could dream for him. He asked me if the dream had provided me with insight or a solution to the issue. I had received some guidance, so I shared it with him.

Later that day he phoned me. He said that the information I had given him had provided a perfect solution to the problem!

This exciting and unexpected experience urged me to explore the concept of dreaming for others. I added the following exercise to my Dream Workshops:

- The participants are formed into pairs, for a "homework" assignment. Each person is directed to dream for her partner, for as many nights as desired, until the next week's session.

- Next, each person gives written permission for the other to dream for her. This step serves two purposes.

   First, it sets the intention to dream. Second, it indicates that the information received will be held in confidence. It will only be shared with her partner, and the class—if permission is given to share with the latter.

Then, each partner writes down a question that she would like an answer to. She does not reveal that question to her partner, until after the dream is shared, during the next class.

This exercise consistently produces amazing results. The participants are always delighted to learn that they can dream for another. Not only that, they are often amazed to learn that they can often provide an answer to their partner's question.

This exercise has become a favorite and intriguing part of my Dream Workshops. The success rate for this exercise seems to be about 90-95%!

If you wish to try this exercise with a friend, please ensure that he wishes to participate. A high degree of trust is essential to the act of dreaming for another. Each participant must feel confident that the gleaned information will be respected and held in confidence.

Precognitive Dreams

Precognitive dreams have been described as a special type of extra perception (ESP). These dreams have also been called dream divinations.

Plenty has been written on this subject. A few of my favorite books are: The Dream Encyclopedia by James Lewis, The Donning International Encyclopedic Psychic Dictionary by June Bletzer, and Harper's Encyclopedia of Mystical and Paranormal Experience.

Characteristics of Precognitive Dreams

 These dreams are quite common; they can be experienced by anyone.

 An event is experienced, in the dream, before it occurs in the dreamer's waking life.

 The dreams often seem quite trivial although at times, the information is significant.

- ⚬ There is usually little or no symbolism.

- ⚬ They generally predict the future, but they can also relate to your current waking life.

- ⚬ Events from home, work or play can become part of a precognitive dream. For example, you could have a dream in which you longed for freedom. Then, the next week you find yourself out of work.

- ⚬ An absence of emotions. Sometimes, emotions are elicited; but they aren't usually personalized. A detached interest in the dream's events is more typical.

- ⚬ Dreams that are filled with strong emotions usually mean that the dream is about some issue in your waking life.

- ⚬ Information can be fragmented; that is, it can come to you in pieces, generally in the same dream, rather than over a series of dreams. Sometimes, the dream contains a complete scenario.

To help determine if the events of the dream could occur, you might ask yourself: "who, what, where, when and why" questions, after you awaken.

Once again, I urge you to keep a Dream Journal. Describing your dreams, in writing, will help you to identify and differentiate between precognitive and "normal" dreams. It will also lend validation to them; you can refer to your journal after an event and verify that you had been alerted to it, in your dreams.

You may be interested to learn that a sense of déjà vu is probably due to a precognitive dream. Déjà vu is the feeling, in your waking life, that you have previously experienced an event.

Now, Rod and Karin and I will discuss precognitive dreams.

> **Karin:** I often have precognitive dreams; they are generally about normal, everyday events. I think the reason is because I suppress my spiritual side during the day. I work in a corporate environment with "left-brained" colleagues. They aren't very receptive to the idea of the value of dreams.

My dreams allow me to fully express and experience my spiritual nature. I recognize when a dream is precognitive, simply by the very strong sense of *knowing*, when I wake up.

Rod: I tend to have precognitive dreams when upcoming events could be shocking and destabilizing. It's as if the dream's purpose is to say "this is what's going to happen, so do not get upset".

Precognitive dreams tend to be previews for my waking life. They allow me to anticipate events; then to adjust my behavior, reactions or emotions ahead of time.

Irene: Surprisingly, I rarely have precognitive dreams. I believe that this is because of my work as a clairvoyant. All day long, I predict future events.

Therefore, my dream state is a rest and release state. It's a time in which I don't have to be concerned about the future.

In the precognitive dreams that I do have, I'm usually answering the phone or turning on the TV. From that, I'll get an auditory or visual message.

A few days before the infamous terrorist attacks in New York on September 11, 2001, I dreamed of televisions blaring around the world. I saw people watching those TVs; they were in states of shock.

On the morning of the attacks, I woke up feeling extremely upset. I turned on the TV and saw a plane crash into The World Trade Center. I knew that the events in my dream were materializing.

Each dreamer has a unique way of receiving messages in precognitive dreams. Here is one of Rod's:

> *I had a dream about two people in my life.*
>
> *Both would get cancer. The dream occurred about two months before they were diagnosed.*
>
> *The dream was lucid. I was in a dialogue with my guides.*
>
> *The last thing that one of them said to me was: "there is only enough time to mention the cancers".*
>
> *At that point I woke up.*

Irene: What did you feel or do about the information?

Rod: I knew that the cancers were going to strike; they were inevitable. I also knew that I could not do anything about them. I concluded that the information was for me to know, but not to share.

Irene: What do you think was the message or reason for the dream?

Rod: I think it was an educational dream. I was surprised to learn that I could receive this type of information. Finally, I had proof that I could talk to my guides and that they were there for me.

Irene: What emotions did you feel when you realized that two people whom you knew were going to succumb to this disease? Did you feel the urge to tell them?

Rod: As bizarre as this may sound, I was so totally amazed at the dream that I was actually elated. My emotions were high and positive.

I did not feel that it was a message for me to deliver, because the two people weren't identified. It was simply an informative message, for me, that the cancers and subsequent deaths were destined.

How precise is a precognitive dream? Can you trust it?

A precognitive dream, just like any other, must be properly analyzed in order to identify its real message and meaning. Thoroughly explore your dream. Ensure that you understand the symbols and their meanings before you share the message. This is particularly important if there is a hint of impending danger or some other negative event in the message. A thorough analysis could result in a different interpretation, than that of a first impression. Take your time!

What is the timeline? Are you sure that it is immediate?

There may be a clue in the dream about when the event will occur. This could be a watch, a clock, the seasons or a mention of the word time (as occurred in Rod's dream). Note: Remember I dreamt of televisions blaring around the world (p 143) and the time element associated with television is that of current events, news in the now, and that is what made me turn on the television as soon as I got up.

I had the following dream about my father's death. At the time of the dream, he was in a hospital. He was scheduled for surgery on both of his lungs.

I dreamed that my father could not breathe and that he was dying.

I heard a clock ticking very loudly. I watched it and saw the hands begin to move very quickly.

I woke up in a sweat and feeling very upset. I knew that he would soon die.

I called the hospital. The nurses connected me to my father; he sounded fine.

Nevertheless, I trusted the message in my dream. I hung up, knowing that he would not survive.

He died that night.

The ticking clock indicated that time was passing for something or someone. In this case, it was my father's time on earth. The accelerated movement of the clock's hands symbolized that his time was quickly running out.

Do you know whom the message is for? Do you know what you should do about it?

The message in a precognitive dream doesn't always have to be delivered. The intent of sharing these types of dreams is not to demonstrate psychic capabilities. Rather, it is to be of help to others.

Not everyone wants to hear about future events; think, before you share your findings. First, log and carefully analyze your dreams. Keep in mind that dreams can be interpreted in a number of ways.

Unless there is a sign or clue that indicates that you need to act, hold your counsel. You probably do not need to say or do anything. You'll recall that Rod had concluded this about his precognitive dream.

Sometimes, the dream's message is intended only for you. It could be that your attention needs to be focused on a particular situation. The dream could be preparing you to cope with it, as did Rod's dream.

The dream could also be alerting you to be prepared to offer someone assistance, when it is needed. Alternately, there could be a learning opportunity, for you, in the dream. Rod concluded that he learned that he could communicate with his guides.

Karin shared this precognitive dream and her reactions to it.

I had a dream in which my co-worker was on his way to Winnipeg. He was going to help his father clean his house after a flood. He was going to be away for a long weekend.

Later, in the dream, he had an injured shoulder. He asked me if it was normal to have a headache for days after an injury. I said no and asked him about his injury. He told me that a load of lumber had fallen on his right shoulder.

He pulled away the right side of his shirt and showed me a large wound, on top of his shoulder. The wound was loosely covered with a large square of white surgical dressing.

I told him that his headaches would likely stop after he got *some medicine. I guessed that the doctors didn't know about his shoulder injury. If they had, they would likely have prescribed something for it.*

When I woke, I felt so much concern for him that I told him about my dream. I suggested that he be careful when he helped a friend with an upcoming move.

Nothing happened during the move.

Two years later, on the Labor Day weekend, he complained of shoulder pain. I remembered the dream; I wondered if it had predicted the shoulder pain.

Irene: Karin, have you had other dreams in which there have been major time delays? If so, this may be a pattern for you. Your precognitive dreams may have a long-range vision.

I'd like to point out some clues about time, which were in your dream. There were no clocks, watches or calendars. But, there were some clues about time as well as other things.

The dream concerned a *long* weekend. Winnipeg is a *long* distance away (from Edmonton). Thus, the injury could happen on a *long* weekend, in the distant future—a *long* time from the dream date.

After a flood could also be a clue. It could refer to a literal flood that would happen in Winnipeg (that city is prone to flooding). The flooding could indicate a time when the co-worker would go there.

The *right shoulder* could refer to a future event. The right side of the body is symbolic of the future; the left side indicates the past.

The *lumber falling* on his shoulder could signify a time when he would feel that he had a lot of weight on his shoulders.

Rod: I have another perspective on this dream. Karin, in the dream, your co-worker asked for your opinion. Maybe that was a clue. It could have been telling you to hold your tongue and to wait until he asked you for advice.

Irene: That's a good point, Rod and worthy of consideration.

Thanks Karin. Your dream illustrates that a precognitive dream isn't always what it seems at first glance. It also shows that precognitive dreams can refer to events that will happen in the distant future.

I would like to share a precognitive dream that concerned a stranger. It held a message that I was entrusted to deliver.

> *I dreamed about a woman, who worked in an Optical Store in a shopping mall.*
>
> *The woman lost her job. Then, she moved from the province of Alberta to British Columbia. She also left her boyfriend as he was not the right one for her.*
>
> *The tone of the dream was happy. It was also very vivid.*
>
> *I had the same dream the next night.*

This kind of dream is rare for me; thus, I knew it was significant. Because it concerned everyday events and didn't have a lot of content, nor was I an active participant who had any emotional attachment to the dream, I concluded that it was precognitive.

About three weeks later, I was in a shopping mall. I wanted to get my glasses adjusted, so I walked into an Optical Outlet. The woman who was working in the store was the woman in my dream!

A hundred questions went through my mind, while I waited to be served. Basically, I wondered if I should tell her about the dream. I hesitated because momentarily I doubted my interpretation. I knew that I had to take responsibility for what could happen, if I told her about it.

Mentally, I reviewed the dream. I arrived at the conclusion that the information in the dream was not harmful. In fact, it could be good news for her. I decided to trust my intuition and tell her about the dream. I wanted to see what would evolve.

We chatted while she adjusted my glasses. I started asking "innocent" questions about her job. She told me that the store was going to close and that she would soon be out of a job.

At that point, I told her about the dream. She was intrigued and wondered if anything good could come from it. I asked her to have faith in the dream's message and requested that she stay in touch with me.

A few weeks later, she phoned to tell me that she had accepted a job in Victoria, British Columbia. She added that she had broken up with her boyfriend. She was thrilled with the events that were unfolding in her life. She said the dream had given her faith and removed her fear and anxiety.

If I hadn't shared the dream, she may not have broken up with her boyfriend and accepted the job in British Columbia. The dream had given her the courage to take a huge leap of faith. She told me that she was very happy and had no regrets.

Both this dream and the one about my father's death were important for me. They re-affirmed who I was and validated my abilities. Further, they confirmed that I needed to continue my work as a clairvoyant and dream interpreter.

Lucid Dreaming

Lucid dreaming is a specific type of dreaming. It forms a bridge between your waking consciousness and your dream state.

In lucid dreams, some event triggers your awareness that you are in a dream; then, you become an active participant. You have the ability to ask questions, to make choices and to influence the action and outcome. This contrasts with most dreams; in those, you are an observer.

Karin had this lucid dream:

> *I was on a moonlit bicycle ride with a co-worker. Everything was so vivid and clear. I could hear the crunch of gravel under our tires. I could feel the peaceful stillness as we cycled through a sleeping neighborhood.*
>
> *I told my co-worker that we were together in a dream. He asked me how I knew that. I replied that we would encounter something unusual and it would confirm that we were in a dream. I added that we would have created it with our minds.*
>
> *I looked up at the sky to see if the moon or stars were different. The constellations were exactly as I knew them in my waking life.*
>
> *We cycled to the crest of a hill and looked down the other side. There before us was a magical, sparkling, cartoon-like village.*
>
> *I excitedly exclaimed: "look, we created that!"*

As you can see from Karin's dream, lucid dreams have a conscious awareness to them. They are usually very vivid and are filled with deliberate actions. It is almost like watching the plot of a movie unfold.

Lucid dreams are not commonly experienced. However, those who have them seem to have them quite frequently. I have noticed that women seem to have more lucid dreams than men do. Similarly, those who meditate seem to have more lucid dreams, than those who don't.

Almost anyone can learn to lucid dream. I teach the following exercises in my Dream Workshops. I'm confident that they will help you learn how to make lucid dreaming a part of your dream experiences.

1. Auto Suggestion.

Several times throughout the day, stare at your hands. At the same time, tell yourself that when you see your hands in a dream, they will be the trigger that will remind you that you are dreaming. From that point, you can take control of your dream.

One reason that I suggest using your hands, as a trigger, is because they are always with you. Similarly, other body parts are always with you. Thus, you can pinch your nose, wiggle your toes, or touch your ears or some other body part. Use anything that seems an appropriate and convenient trigger.

> **Karin:** Your technique of hand staring worked for me. I practiced it as soon as I became aware of it. Then, the first time that I saw myself in a dream, I looked at my hands.

Immediately, I was aware that I could begin to control the events of the dream. I was so excited! It was so empowering to realize that I could bring my waking consciousness into a dream.

2. Use of Objects.

Objects can also be used as triggers to initiate lucid dreaming. Suitable objects include: eye glasses, pens, coins, stones, photographs and amulets. Use anything that you wish.

Crystals make good triggers. Rose quartz is known as the love stone. You may wish to gaze at it before bed, while asking a question about a relationship. Then, you may see the stone appear in your dream, as well as your new love. Go ahead and introduce yourself!

3. Waking Up from a Dream.

If you become distressed during a lucid or other type of dream, you can wake yourself up. Simply look for your trigger object and take control of the dream.

Alternately, create something that will enable you to take control of the action. A door or window could provide an escape route. A ray of light could surround and protect you.

One of my clients loves superheroes. He created a special character to rescue him from disturbing dreams. After the rescue, they go off on a special adventure!

Another client uses a helicopter. Each time that he has a dream that he wants to escape from, a helicopter comes and rescues him.

Lucid dreaming empowers you to work with your dreams.

When lucid dreaming, you can stop the action and ask questions such as the following:

- Is the person I am with the perfect mate for me?
- Am I making the right career choice?
- What do I need to know about my life right now?
- Is this a good time to travel?
- Are you my guide? While lucid dreaming, you can ask your guides for direction and advice on any aspect of your life.

Think of all the possibilities that lucid dreaming can offer. You can create characters, backgrounds and story lines. You can also explore creative ideas and participate in wonderful adventures.

I would like to share a lucid dream that I had. It is one of my favorite.

I was sitting in a warm, sunny meadow. The flowers and blue sky were enchanting.

I saw a beautiful, white horse emerge from the forest; it cantered towards me. I realized that it was Pegasus, the mystical, winged horse.

At that point, I looked down at my hands and realized I was dreaming.

Pegasus came up to me. I understood his thoughts and he understood mine. I asked him if he would take me for a ride. He agreed and I climbed onto his back. He magically and smoothly lifted into the air. We went faster and faster and flew into outer space. I knew that I was safe. I also knew that I could do anything, go anywhere or change anything in the dream. I spent the entire dream playing in the universe with Pegasus. It was so mystical and magical; I didn't want the dream to end.

Karin: Sometimes, in lucid dreaming, something unusual or bizarre triggers an awareness that you are in the dream state. If you hadn't used your hands as a trigger, perhaps Pegasus could have been the trigger.

Rod: Irene, once you became aware that you were dreaming, you took control of the dream. That was when you asked Pegasus to take you for a ride.

Irene: It was very magical; there were no limitations. I did not need oxygen to go into space and I had absolutely no fear. I could do anything that I wanted!

Rod: That's because all aspects of physical reality were suspended, while you were in the dream state.

Karin: Therefore, you could create anything you wished to during the lucid dream.

Irene: I didn't have much emotional attachment to anything in the dream. I had the power to change things; I didn't take any fears or insecurities with me. I was beyond my waking limitations.

Sometimes dreams can be of more than one type. Let's take a second look at Rod's precognitive dream about the cancers. It was also a lucid dream.

> *I had a dream about two people in my life. Both would get cancer. The dream occurred about two months before they were diagnosed.*
>
> *The dream was lucid. I was in a dialogue with my guides.*
>
> *The last thing that one of them said to me was: "there is only enough time to mention the cancers".*
>
> *At that point I woke up.*

Irene: Sometimes lucid dreams have a purpose or a connection to the physical plane. Rod, because it was a lucid dream, you could have asked your guides if the cancers could be healed. There could have been further dialogue.

Rod: Twice I felt myself waking up, but I decided to stay in the dream, in order to get more information.

Although it was lucid, the dream was almost like a demonstration. Once I knew that I was dreaming, I realized that I was in control of the time that I chose to wake up.

Irene: What did you think was the purpose of the dream? Who was it really for?

Rod: My dad had previously been ill with cancer, so I thought that maybe it was coming back. My aunt's cancer was diagnosed after the dream.

The overriding sense was that the dream was a demonstration. My guides were simply showing me how lucid dreaming worked; the purpose wasn't for me to do anything about the cancers.

Karin: Perhaps the demonstration was also intended to show you that you had no control over the outcome of the cancers. They were events that would definitely occur. So, when they did, they validated your ability to lucid dream.

Irene: Notice that this particular lucid dream did not have a magical theme to it. The dream was realistic; it concerned waking life events.

At the time of Rod's lucid dream, he was in poor health. His anxiety could have created the dream. The cancer could have symbolized his concerns about his health.

Cancer eats away at you; so does fear and worry. If Rod had shared the dream with his relatives, it might have created unnecessary concern and anxiety for them. The dream may have simply been about Rod.

Most of the time, lucid dreams give you a direct message. Karin wanted to validate her spiritual consciousness to one of her co-workers. So, she created a moonlit bicycle ride dream to explain it to him.

Perhaps I wanted an escape from reality. So, I went for a ride on Pegasus to a magical and inspiring place, where there were no limits.

Rod had a health concern. Because he is an analytical thinker, he dreamed of health problems.

There is a distinct quality to lucid dreams. They have unusual clarity and are usually very colorful. In other words, they create a significant impact on your senses.

That vividness is because you take your waking consciousness into the dream. The result is that the dream seems very, very real.

As you can see, lucid dreaming can be powerful, fun and changed on command. Not only can you ask your guides questions, you can ask for healing in lucid dreams. I would like to share one of my experiences with healing in a lucid dream.

One day when I was bending down to lift a heavy garden stone, I hurt my back. That night, when I went to bed, I focused on a request that my body would heal itself. I visualized that my back would be fine in the morning. I kept the thought and image in my mind until I fell asleep. I dreamed.

In the dream, I saw my hands trying to reach around and rub my back. I realized that I was lucid dreaming. I told my arms that they could stretch as much as they needed to in order to rub my back. I felt them stretch; my hands began to rub my back, they put pressure in the right places. I allowed healing to occur. I knew, in the dream, that in the morning my back would be fine. It was!

When you create an intention and empower it with desire, success will surely follow! Apply this concept to lucid dreaming and be prepared to amaze yourself.

Spiritual Dreams

What is a spiritual dream? How do you know you are having one?

I believe that all dreams are spiritual in nature. However, some are more spiritual than others.

Dreams in this category often contain mystical or religious messages. Those messages tend to be very profound. Guides and angels are often present in spiritual dreams.

Sometimes, spiritual dreams reflect the dreamer's core values and beliefs. They can also reflect her questions about unusual events that cannot be explained by science or day-to-day experiences.

Rod: Guides sometimes appear in my spiritual dreams. They are not from this world. The messages that they bring me are mysterious and beyond my knowledge.

Irene: I view dreams as gifts and special messages that come from your soul. They can open up unlimited possibilities for you, if you are able to interpret their messages and follow their guidance.

There is always an element of mysticism or magic to my spiritual dreams. I wake up feeling as if I have been privileged to experience the dream. Sometimes, there is some kind of revelation or enlightenment in the dream.

Karin: My spiritual dreams convey powerful emotions; they come from deep within me. Those dreams are profound, divine and peaceful. There is a sense of sacredness to them.

Irene: Spiritual dreams can make you feel as though your soul has been touched, by something divine.

A spiritual dream caused one of my clients to wake up. She said it felt as if God had touched her; she was so moved and felt so blissful.

Many people feel that dreams must have religious figures or powerful messages before they can be considered spiritual. That is simply not true. Feelings or a sense of awareness, of their special nature, can make them spiritual.

Karin: If you've had a religious upbringing or later adopted a spiritual philosophy, you might encounter a high spiritual being in your dreams.

Those evolved spiritual beings could include: Jesus, Buddha, Mother Mary, an angel or a saint. Or, in your dreams you could visit a spiritual place such as a temple, a church or a pyramid.

Irene: A spiritual dream often has something projecting itself into the dream, something beyond what you could reasonably create. A profound sense of awe, wonder or reverence could be part of such a dream.

A spiritual dream can hold a moment of realization that you are a part of something greater than yourself. That moment could be simple or profound and could bring enlightenment to any situation, whether it is in the past, present or future.

For example, in a dream, you could be watching a family scene. Suddenly, the dynamics of the action or the conversation sheds light on a situation that has long puzzled you. Then, when you wake up, you think: "ah-ha, now I get it".

That "ah-ha" moment could also come through an unexpected waking life experience. Regardless of how it comes, that moment of enlightenment could be so profound that it could change your belief system. That, in turn, could change your life.

Spiritual dreams are often unusual. Frequently, they contain an event that is beyond the range of your normal dream experiences. Such dreams can create a connection with some spiritual being or event. That could be: a guide, an angel or a deceased loved one. The dream could also be precognitive.

One night, when I was about seven years old, I had a dream in which I was in danger. I cannot remember what I was running from, but I can remember that I was crying and very afraid.

Suddenly, I saw an Aboriginal Chief named Red Cloud; he put a ray of light around me. My fear, crying and running immediately ceased. The dream became magical; I felt safe and happy when I woke up.

How did I know it was Red Cloud? I had seen him, in spirit form, standing over my grandfather's (dead) body. I was four years old at the time. Red Cloud told me his name and added that he would *always* be there to watch over me.

Later, when I described how Red Cloud had saved me with a white light, no one except my mother believed me. I did not know it at the time, but that dream was the beginning of my intuitive training. The years of working with Red Cloud had begun.

Rod: In 2001 I had a dream about a fighter pilot, who turned and winked at me. That scene told me that there was an energy projecting itself into my dreams. I knew that that energy was going to become a significant part of my life.

That was the point when I stopped believing and started *knowing*. I never, in a hundred years, could have made up that dream scene. It was completely unlike anything else I had ever dreamed.

Karin: My turning point occurred one morning, while I was driving to work. I had a mystical experience; it was a spontaneous event, I don't know what caused it. Suddenly, I felt a wonderful sense of unity and connection to everything in the world. The birds seemed to speak to me and the earth seemed to breathe.

At that moment, I saw the world with new eyes. I was part of everything around me. It was a very powerful and moving experience; it only lasted a minute, but it changed me forever. My perspective had changed. I wasn't living my life alone; I felt "connected" to everything.

Irene: Every soul and every life has a purpose. Each time that your soul incarnates into physical form, it gains deeper understanding and greater wisdom.

I believe that everyone is here, on earth, to love and serve each other. Each time that you discover more love, compassion, understanding and forgiveness, within yourself, you grow closer to your real purpose in life.

That is how you connect to a higher energy form, which you may call God, spirit, source or some other name. That connection leads to greater inner peace and harmony.

My dreams, especially the spiritual ones, have gifted me in many ways. Through them, I have received profound messages, wonderful insights, wisdom and spiritual growth.

Guides and Angels

Guides

Every person has one or more guides who are assigned, or sometimes chosen, before he is born. As that individual grows and evolves, higher guides—up to nine in a lifetime—are assigned. Some, or all, of those guides stay with the individual until he leaves the physical form. They are always there even if they can't be seen, heard or sensed.

In contrast, angels are spirit beings who are available to assist everyone; they are not assigned to a specific individual. The exception is guardian angels. Each person is assigned a guardian angel; that angel stays with him for the duration of that physical life.

Guides often appear in your dreams, where they are generally easy to spot. All that you have to do is look for a face or person who seems familiar, but whom you can't quite identify. Often, that familiar being is on the sidelines, where he (or she) observes your actions. If your guide sees that you need help, he will attempt to make a connection through the use of a symbol or by speaking directly to you.

In one of my dreams, I turned down a road that was under construction. A worker stopped me; he told me that the road would not be open for some time. He suggested that I take a short cut that was just behind me and to the right. I thanked him and turned around.

I knew that the road was symbolic of my life's journey and the worker was my guide. He was telling me that, in some part of my waking life, I was headed in the wrong direction. He was encouraging me to take a faster and easier route.

I didn't have to take my guide's advice. (Remember, you always have choices.) I could have waited until the road was open, even if that would have resulted in a delay.

A choice to wait could have indicated that I was stalling for time about something in my waking life. Because I took his advice, it indicated that I was ready to make a decision and change direction in some area of my waking life.

Guides often appear in your dreams when they are least expected. Similarly, they often play unusual or unexpected roles just like my guide did when he appeared as a construction worker.

If you are receptive to the idea that your guides can appear at any time, it will be easier for you to work with them. And, you'll be able to more easily relate the dream's message to your waking life.

Why do guides appear in your dreams?

Your guides appear in your dreams to offer you peace of mind, hope, strength and the assurance that you are never alone. They are there to help you to advance as a spiritual being. They also come when you ask them to, whenever you need their guidance or advice.

Your guides' assistance comes in the form of messages and directions. Not listening to or heeding those messages is usually due to fear or disbelief that they are with you. Arrogance, an attitude that you do not need help from anyone or anything, can interfere with your guides' offers of help.

Understanding your guides' messages requires patience and an open mind. Every time that you attempt to understand and heed their guidance, your wisdom grows. As your wisdom grows, your attitude and outlook toward all people and all things will change. It will become more compassionate and benevolent. That, in turn, will reflect a more universal consciousness.

I frequently call upon my guides for help. For instance, when I wake up and wish to go back into a dream, I will ask for a guide to be there with me. Or, I will look for one in the dream, if I felt that she had been there while I was dreaming.

I do the same thing while lucid dreaming. I look for a guide to assist me to play out the dream's action, in any manner that I desire.

Ask to meet your guides and angels, in the quiet moments that occur, just before you drift off to sleep. This invites their appearance and increases the chance that they will appear.

Meeting Your Guides

Your guides will appear when they feel that you are ready to meet them. One way that they make contact is through the use of symbols.

Those symbols can appear in your waking life, as well as in your dreams. Repetitive symbols can be major clues that your guides are nearby. Please pay attention to those symbols.

One of my clients discovered that a monarch butterfly represented one of her guides. It consistently appeared whenever she grieved the death of someone, who had been close to her. She was always comforted by its presence.

Guides can appear as themselves, as well as symbols.

When I first met my guide, Red Cloud, I was a four-year old child. He told me, with great emphasis, to cover my eyes. Just as I did that a rooster flew at me and pecked my face, hands and head. When the rooster was gone, I looked around and saw Red Cloud.

Karin met her guide in a dream; she shared that dream in "The Body in Dreams" section. You will recall that it was an Aboriginal elder, who took away her headache.

Rod's guide first appeared as a blue man who was flying an F–18 Eagle fighter plane. Rod felt that he should combine the symbolism of the blue man and the eagle aircraft. From that, he arrived at the name of "Blue Eagle" for his guide.

Rod felt that the jet and the man also meant that Blue Eagle was a warrior for peace and empowerment. Because Rod made that connection, he can now look for Blue Eagle whenever he dreams, meditates or needs the inner strength that his guides bring. Similar images or symbols could also indicate that Blue Eagle is nearby and ready to assist Rod in whatever way he can.

Guides Can Change—They are Not Constant

I hope that you have accepted the concept that your guides are always present and eager to be of assistance. Please be aware that your guides can change. I was unprepared when I learned that my guides were changing.

One day I had a psychic reading; the reader was a very gifted and mystical man. He told me that Red Cloud needed to let me go. I was stunned.

I had known Red Cloud for most of my life; I didn't want to let him go. I felt a sense of loss and grief, similar to that of losing a parent.

The reader said to me: "just as a father sends a child off to college, it is now time for Red Cloud to send you off to a place of higher spiritual learning. There are, more powerful and masterful guides to help you along your spiritual path". The reader told me to meditate on this and to be open and ready to receive a new guide.

One day, during a meditation, I saw a beautiful Tibetan monk on a bridge. He was walking toward me. He stopped in the middle of the bridge and held out a hand to me. He said "my name is Master Wan Que; it is time, come with me".

My new guide had come to work with me. He is still a part of my life. Some time later, a colleague in my waking life, told me that Master Wan Que's name meant "the one source".

I learned, through my experiences with Master Wan Que, that some guides are more than just guides; they are spiritual teachers. To illustrate this, I will briefly describe my relationships with Red Cloud and Master Wan Que; they are distinctly different.

Whenever Red Cloud was with me, he would usually point to a symbol or a clue to help me understand a message that he was trying to convey. There was generally little or no conversation.

In contrast, my encounters with Master Wan Que are filled with deep and meaningful conversations. On the spiritual plane, we go for long walks and I ask him hundreds of questions. I listen with awe and respect to his answers; they are full of wisdom. He also brings other spiritual teachers to me.

Guides and spiritual teachers are sometimes connected to the Ascended Masters or more powerful angels. Ascended Masters are exceptional spiritual teachers who, at one time, had walked on the earth. Among these are Jesus Christ, Buddha and Mohammed.

How do you connect with your guides?

One of the most common reasons that clients come to see me is so that I can help them to connect with their guides. What those clients don't realize is that they have already met their guides. They are just not aware of it, because the connections are so subtle.

I am able to forge a connection with spirit guides during a *Soul Reading*. During the reading, I invite my client's guides to make a connection with me. Then, I relay their messages to my client along with the guide's name and often the reason for the connection. *Soul Readings* can help my client to identify her life purpose and to glimpse into significant past lives.

You can ask your guides to come to you in your dreams. To do this, you must set the intention that you would like to meet them. Do this during the day and again immediately before you drift into sleep.

Please recall that receiving answers to questions, in your dreams, may take more than one night. Similarly, the quest to meet your guides can take more than one dream.

Try not to get discouraged if they don't immediately appear. It may take several nights in a row of focused intention before you are successful. Be persistent, I am confident that your perseverance will be rewarded.

Be aware that your guides may not always come to you in human form.

(Key #6: People or animals are not always "who they are" in the dream.)

For example, in a dream a dog could appear out of nowhere and be completely out of context. The dog may try to get you to follow him. In the morning, you may not recall the experience, even though you may have gone to someplace meaningful with the dog. You may only recall that there was a beautiful dog in your dream. This example illustrates that not every encounter with a guide is mystical or seemingly significant.

Your guides can also come to you during meditations or periods of quiet reflection. Whether in dreams, meditations or in quiet moments, keep in mind that they may not appear as you think they will.

A clue that they are present is an increased awareness of certain things. Those things could be repeated symbols, messages and familiar characters. Those characters often assist you in your dreams, in spite of the fact that you don't know them.

If you think you have identified someone or some thing that could be a guide or guided message, ensure that you express your gratitude. Thanking your guide for the information will encourage more frequent visits.

When that guide appears again, ask for his (or her) name. Then, in future encounters, you can greet him by name. Do not be discouraged if the guide doesn't offer a name; the time may not be right for you to know it. Rest assured, he will reveal his name when the time and place are right.

Angels

It is wonderful to be able to recognize guides or angels, when they appear in dreams. This helps you to decode the dream's message. This is particularly true when there are bizarre symbols or fragmented dream scenes.

Angels can appear in ways other than in dreams. They can come as animals, birds or other creatures in your waking life.

Archangel Michael is a powerful guide and angel; his mission is to care for and assist all humans. The first time I saw him, I was five years old; I've seen him many times since then.

One Christmas, he appeared in my home; I captured his image on film. That picture is one of my cherished possessions; I love to show it to my clients and friends.

Whenever I feel in need of Archangel Michael's guidance, I ask him to visit me in my dreams; invariably he appears. He also visits me in my waking life; during those times he appears as an eagle. He always soars close to me.

The first time I associated Archangel Michael with an eagle was shortly after my mother's death. I was deeply grieving her passing. I missed her so much; I needed to know that she was in heaven and at peace. I looked up at the sky and prayed for a sign that she was okay.

An eagle appeared overhead and soared close to me. It seemed to look directly at me. It flew away and then circled back. Once again, it soared over my head. I was amazed, but didn't over-analyze the event. Nevertheless, I wondered why an eagle was in the area.

This incident happened when I was sitting outside, at the Edmonton International Airport. My understanding was that birds are safety hazards for aircraft, thus are usually kept away, or stay away, from airports.

A few weeks later, I had a dream about angels. In the dream, I asked Archangel Michael to give me a sign that my mother was okay and that he had heard my prayers.

As the dream unfolded, I saw myself in my car that was parked on the side of a road. I saw the shape of an angel appear in the sky. As I watched, the angel transformed itself into an eagle.

The eagle then soared close to me, just as it had at the airport. From that moment on, a soaring eagle became the symbol of Archangel Michael, for me.

You may have a different symbol for him. Additionally, an eagle may mean something different for you. For some people, an eagle symbolizes power, freedom and a great spirit. Remember, you must assign personal meanings to symbols; that is of utmost importance.

The appearance of the eagle at the airport and in my dream was very significant. At the time of the airport eagle sighting, I was not working as a clairvoyant and medium. I was filled with doubt about whether or not I wanted to continue with that kind of work.

Seeing and dreaming about the eagle and understanding that it was Archangel Michael gave me great comfort. The whole experience assured me that my mother was in a better place. It also put me back on my career path. I realized that my true calling is working with the spirit world, in order to help others.

Since the dream and airport experience, I have repeatedly seen eagles in my dreams and waking life. They always bring me comfort and insight.

Connecting with Deceased Loved Ones

There is a very thin veil dividing the physical and spiritual worlds. As a Medium, I focus on that veil in order to connect with souls who have passed from the living world.

In a similar way, your higher self finds it relatively easy to connect and communicate with the spirit world while you are asleep. During your waking hours, those connections are more difficult to establish.

Your higher self can connect with your deceased loved ones through your dreams. In those dreams, your loved ones appear as "visitations". This is the most common type of first contact. They can also appear as ghostly forms in your waking life.

There is a difference between visitations and the appearance of deceased loved ones in ordinary dreams. It is fairly easy to tell the difference.

When your loved ones are part of an ordinary dream scene, they act as other characters do; nothing seems out of the ordinary. Sometimes your subconscious uses their characteristics to represent something else; in other words, they are merely symbols.

In contrast, when they come as a visitation, they often appear suddenly and unexpectedly. They usually seem brighter and often have a soft glow of light around them. They rarely speak; they simply stand there and offer you silent comfort.

They want to reassure you that they are doing well in the spirit world. Sometimes they appear as partial images; that is, just as a face or an upper body. Their presence is strongest during the first year after they have "passed".

Be aware that some souls, who have passed, do not feel the same way. They are happy in the spirit world and simply do not feel the need to re-connect with the living world.

Visitations often occur on or near significant dates. These include birthdays, anniversaries and dates of their passing. If you have a dream that contains a visitation, carefully examine it. There may be a connection between that visitation and something in your waking life.

Similarly, whenever you see deceased family members or friends in your dreams, take some time to reflect on your memories of them. Such reflections could offer clues as to why they have entered your dreams. They may have come to help you resolve some issue in your waking life.

Karin had a very powerful dream, on the night that her grandmother died. It was brief, but accurate. It illustrates how spirits can relay messages to living beings. Here is the dream:

> *I dreamed that my grandmother had given me her watch.*
> *I had asked her to stop the watch the minute that she died,*
> *so that I would know exactly when it happened.*
>
> *At the moment that it stopped, the phone rang; it woke me from the dream.*
>
> *My sister called; she told me that Grandma had just died.*

There had been a strong emotional connection between Karin and her grandmother. The dream reflected that bond.

Karin had asked her grandmother to send her a sign that would indicate the moment when she died. What clearer sign could there be than her grandmother's watch? It clearly symbolized that her life had "stopped".

What about pets? They too can "speak" to you through your dreams.

As previously discussed, in Part Six, animals can appear in dreams. Deceased pets try to bring comfort to their masters.

An example of this is the dream that I had when a friend's cat, Sushi, died. My friend was deeply upset by Sushi's death. Here is the dream:

> *I saw four little kittens playing. Sushi was on*
> *the sidelines watching them. Suddenly, my*
> *deceased sister's face appeared and smiled. Then,*
> *Sushi went and joined the kittens.*

The dream told me Sushi was in heaven and that she was happy. The dream was made more powerful by the appearance of my sister's face.

Her appearance confirmed that Sushi had gone to heaven. I had always believed that pets go to the "other side" to await their master's "home coming". My friend was thrilled when I shared my dream's message with her.

A Referral from Spirit!

One day, in the spring of 2004, two people came to me hoping to make a connection with their brother. He had died, in an industrial accident, shortly before the reading.

Within moments, I had connected to their brother. His spirit wanted to communicate, through me, the circumstances of the accident. He was able to offer those answers and comfort.

The most amazing aspect (for me) of this experience was what unfolded after the reading. I asked the pair how they happened to come to see me. One of them related that he had been told to come and see me. The "person" who had done the urging was the brother from the spirit world!

I wondered aloud if I had known him as a client prior to his death; that wasn't the case. One of the clients told me that a short time after the funeral, his deceased brother appeared in a dream. He told the dreamer to "go and see Irene Martina".

The client said that he was barely awake; nevertheless, he managed to write my name on a piece of paper. The time was 3:00 A.M. That didn't surprise me; most spirits visit around that time.

The next morning, my client sat down at his computer and accessed the Internet. He typed in my name to see what would happen. He was astonished to learn that I existed and that we lived in the same city!

I'm always amazed at the innovative ways that spirits send messages to the living. Usually, they aren't as clear as this one. Regardless, I'm pleased to know that communication between the spirit and earthly worlds can be initiated from either side.

Spirits can "drop in" unannounced.

Spirits don't always appear, in your dreams or your waking life, to help you resolve an issue. Sometimes, they simply appear because they have an opportunity to do so.

They are, after all, your family, friends or guides. They feel that they can drop in unexpectedly and will be welcomed. Do not be frightened by their appearance; greet them as though they were there, in the flesh.

> **Rod:** Why can't we pull in famous people, at a whim, just as we can attract loved ones? I would love to have Marilyn Monroe appear in my dreams!
>
> **Irene:** That's a good question; I can only answer from my experience. I have had celebrities appear in my dreams and in my *Medium Readings*, both as themselves and as symbolism.
>
> I can recall two readings in particular. In the first, a family wanted to hear from their adult son, who had died.
>
> In the reading, I heard Frank Sinatra singing. I told the family that I was hearing Frank sing. They exclaimed that their son had been a big Sinatra fan. I told them which song Frank was singing; it happened to be their son's favorite. They added that, because of what I'd said they knew that their son's spirit was in the room, with us.
>
> I couldn't decide if Frank was visiting us or if I was merely hearing his voice. Then, suddenly I saw him briefly appear behind my clients - he winked at me and then he vanished!
>
> On another occasion another well-known musician, Elvis Presley, participated in a reading. He prefaced that visit by one in a dream, which I had during the night before the reading.
>
> In that dream, Elvis was on the sidelines. He smiled at me and told me that he would see me tomorrow. At the time I did not know exactly what he meant. I thought and hoped that he would appear in a reading. I excitedly looked forward to the next day.
>
> That day a woman came to see me; she wanted to make a connection to a sister who had committed suicide. About ten minutes into the reading, I heard Elvis singing. I did not see him, but I certainly felt his presence in the room.
>
> It turned out that my client's sister had been an avid Elvis fan. During the

reading, the deceased sister's spirit told me that Elvis was there, near her, and that he was singing. She added that she was so happy because she had met him, in the spirit world.

My client and I laughed at this information. Then, I heard Elvis begin to sing *Peace in the Valley*. My client declared that that song had been one of her sister's favorites.

My client passionately felt that her sister was telling her that she had finally found "peace". She believed that her sister was saying that she was happy. My client left with a sense of serenity.

So, to more concisely answer Rod's question, about pulling in celebrities, I believe that they enter your dreams, meditations and readings for a specific purpose. I believe that they appear to offer some kind of assistance. They also offer validation that a connection between a client and his loved one has been made.

Perhaps, the rare appearances of celebrities make their messages more powerful. Celebrities, just like other spirits, stay close to their family groups in the spirit world. They don't entertain and act as celebrities, as they did while in the physical world.

Past Lives

How many of you can say with certainty that you have (or have not) previously lived in more life times? Hundreds of people re-live what seem to be past life experiences. Can you remember a time when you lived in another body?

In the past several decades, interest in the idea of reincarnation has grown in the western world. Many hypnotists, therapists, energy workers and others who are interested in reincarnation have written books and articles on the subject. They have documented amazing accounts of their clients' past life memories, sometimes with proof of those lives.

Some of my favorite books about past lives are: *Many Lives, Many Masters* by Brian Weiss, *Coming From the Light* by Sarah Hinze, *Across Time and Death* by Jenny Cockell, *Old Souls: Compelling Evidence from Children who Remember Past Lives* by Thomas Shroder and *Practical Guide to Past Life Memories* by Richard Webster.

Memories from your past life times are recorded in your soul's history. Those memories can be accessed through dreams, hypnotism and waking life triggers. (An example of a waking life trigger is related later under the section of reincarnation and dreams; it is the story of the boy and a horse.)

Memories of past life times can be clear and persistent, particularly in the very young. This is especially true in cultures where the belief in past lives is eagerly embraced. India is one example.

The following true story describes a young boy's memories of a past life.

My Other Mommy

A woman brought her three and a half year old son to see me. The reason was because he frequently spoke about his "other mommy", whom he believed he had had before he was born to his present day mother. This bothered the woman a lot, particularly because she was a devout Christian. She did not believe in the possibility of past lives.

I asked the woman to wait in another room while I interviewed the child. (Children usually speak to me more freely when their parents are not present.)

After I had established a bond with the boy, I asked him to tell me about his other mommy. His eyes lit up and he happily related stories from a previous life.

He told me his (then) name and the names of his other mommy and daddy. He also told me where he had lived.

I asked him how he died. He related that he had died in a car accident when he was four years old. He gave me the date. I then asked him if he liked living with his present day mommy. He replied that he did; he said that he loved his mommy and was happy living with her.

After the interview, I gave the woman an audio-cassette recording of the session. I suggested that she research the names, address and accident date that her son had given me.

A few weeks later, the woman phoned me. She told me that she had verified that a child had died, in a car accident, on the date that her son had given me. She added that they had driven by the address her son had quoted. Apparently, he recognized the house. He excitedly exclaimed that it was where he used to live, with his other mommy and daddy.

This story illustrates how details of a past life can be confirmed by using present day information and anecdotal evidence. Police records, newspapers, magazines, books and Internet searches can all be used to verify details of past life claims.

A past life dream and how it was connected to my waking life.

My past life dream brought great insight not only to me, but also to others who were involved. Here is that (true) story.

When I was about 10 years old, I dreamed that I had been a monk, during the Spanish Inquisition. The dream was very real and very frightening.

In the dream, I was in charge of an underground tunnel. Its purpose was to save people from imprisonment in some chambers that were located below an old monastery. Prisoners there were being cruelly tortured by Catholic Priests.

While in the dream state, I felt as if I knew some of the dream people in my waking life. However, I could not make any firm associations. In the dream I was caught and tortured. At that point, I woke up.

I thought that it was a strange dream; it was unlike any of my usual dreams. I told my mother about it; she closely questioned me about events in my waking life. She was trying to determine if I had received a nightmare message and if it was connected to my (then) current reality.

The dream recurred sporadically for many months. Neither my mother nor I could associate the dream to anything in my waking life. Nevertheless, we knew that eventually its significance would be revealed to us. That proved to be the case.

One day at school, I was sent to the principal's office. I was questioned about some damage that had been done in the Girls' washroom. I knew a little bit about the vandalism and the possible culprits. I had heard some other students discussing the incident.

I hadn't been involved, thus I wasn't sure of the facts. In addition, I didn't want to "rat" on anyone, so I didn't identify any of the rumored vandals.

Suddenly, as I stood in front of the principal's desk, a most peculiar sensation came over me. I had an eerie feeling that I had been in similar positions, with her, many times before.

It seemed as though I was seeing different faces superimposed on her face. I felt as though I was no longer in the current time period. In a matter of seconds, I felt a strange and intense connection to my dreams of the Spanish Inquisition.

To make the story short, the principal was convinced that I had been involved in the vandalism. She wouldn't believe that I was innocent. She strapped my hands, with a piece of leather, until they were raw and bleeding.

When I got home and my mother saw my hands, she took me to a hospital for treatment. She then laid charges against the principal and withdrew me from the school. The principal was later fired.

A few nights later, I had the dream again. On that occasion, I recognized the principal as one of the priests who had caught and tortured me. I woke up screaming. That was the last time that I had that dream.

In retrospect, I believe that my dreams had been precognitive. Everything that I experienced in the principal's office felt real, yet at the same time, surreal. I experienced the same feelings in the principal's office, as I had in the dreams.

My mother was convinced that the dream concerned one of my past lives. She believed that there was a probable soul connection between the principal and me. Some unfinished business was being played out in our waking lives.

My mother also thought that I could have been dealing with some kind of karmic debt. (See more on karmic debt later.) Whatever the reason, the whole experience was terrifying and yet powerful because of the information that it held. I have never forgotten those dreams or my experiences with the principal.

Nightmares + A Past Life Reading = Spiritual Healing

I have done dozens of *Past Life* readings. In virtually all of them, my clients experienced some "ah ha" moments. They were able to understand the significance of some experience in a prior life. They were then able to connect it to something in their current lives. In other words, a spiritual understanding and healing had occurred.

Other benefits from such "ah ha" connections include the understanding of personal strengths and weaknesses and insight into personal problems.

To illustrate the power of a past life understanding, I will now relate a story of one of my clients who had been tormented, for years, by nightmares of snakes.

I asked him what the dream symbol of a snake meant to him. He replied that it was "something very scary". I advised him that sometimes snakes signify betrayal and torture.

He was motivated to participate in a Past Life reading. During the first phase of his journey, he saw himself as a twelve-year old boy, living on a farm in Iowa. He was playing field ball with two other boys.

Suddenly, the ball went out-of-bounds and fell into an old well. The boy who owned the ball was very upset. He knew that he would be in trouble, with his father, if he went home without it. The well didn't seem very deep, so the boys discussed how they could retrieve it.

At that point, my client became quite anxious. I asked him if he wanted to come back to the present; that is, to terminate the session. He replied that he didn't, chiefly because he recognized one of the boys as someone in his current life.

Next, my client, as the twelve-year old boy, looked into the well. He felt one of the other boy's hands on his back. Suddenly, he slipped and fell into the well. Someone screamed in alarm.

At that point, one boy ran to get help while the other stayed to offer emotional support. In the well, my client thrashed about and tried to get out. He heard a noise and saw a snake near his arm. He became frantic and screamed that there were lots of snakes in the well. He begged for someone to get him out.

The boy who had run for help returned with his father, who had brought a rope. The adult quickly pulled the overwrought boy (my client) out of the well.

After he had calmed down, my twelve year old client accused the boy whose hands he had felt on his back, of pushing him into the well. The boy countered that he hadn't pushed; rather, he had been trying to grab my client's belt, to prevent him from falling into the well.

At that point, my client wanted to return to the present time; I quickly brought him back. He was shocked to have discovered that the boy, who he thought had pushed him into the well, was his brother in his current life!

He then added that as far back as he could remember, he had never trusted his brother. He couldn't explain why. He said that his brother had always been perplexed by the mistrust, because he had never done anything to earn it.

Several days later, my client called to tell me that he had shared the tape of the session with his brother. He said that because of the revelations on the tape, they had formed a new relationship. He now trusted his brother and a deep bond was forming between them.

My client joyfully reported that the nightmares had stopped. He added that he felt more confident, peaceful and open. He knew that a deep healing had occurred because of the Past Life session.

What is karma?

Simply put, *karma* is the "Law of Cause and Effect". In other words, each action has a consequence. Thus, some karma is positive and some is negative.

Negative karma can be created by judgment errors, mistakes and bad behavior. Unresolved negative karma is commonly referred to as *Karmic Debt*. Each individual must make restitution for his karmic debts.

The "payback" of the debt can be done in the lifetime in which it was created or in a future life or lives. Said another way, a Karmic Debt can be carried forward from one lifetime to the next. This is done until the debt has been repaid.

Karmic Lessons differ from Karmic Debts. Karmic Lessons can be likened to extra study, tutorials or lessons that you have chosen for a particular lifetime. The purpose of those Karmic Lessons is to help you to develop certain characteristics, attitudes and beliefs that will help you to spiritually evolve.

You may carry one or many Karmic Debts and Karmic Lessons in your current life. Alternately, you may be free of one or both of these forms of karma.

Numerology deals extensively with this subject. You may wish to consult a Numerologist in order to identify and understand any karma that you may have.

What is the purpose of reincarnation?

Reincarnation is the belief that your soul never dies and that it (you) is reborn into a new body time and time again. In each new life you have a new personality and new experiences.

Reincarnation provides your soul with opportunities to spiritually evolve. This evolvement requires experiences and learning that can only be acquired on the physical plane.

From a very young age, I accepted the idea of reincarnation. That was because of my mother's spiritual approach to life and her absolute belief in reincarnation and the evolution of the soul. I recall her stating with great conviction: "if God can bring life back to Mother Earth each spring, surely He would do the same for His greatest creation—human kind!"

How does reincarnation relate to dreams?

Your soul has perfect memories of all of your lifetimes. Sometimes you can be reminded of your history in simple ways, particularly in your dreams.

Dreams that have unusual settings or time references could be related to past life events. These could be something like being on an ancient sailing ship or fighting in a Civil War. Pay close attention to dreams that are set in other times and places. Try and relate the dream symbols or emotions to your present day life.

Three of my clients had had dreams of happy life times in France. Each had furnished her present day home with French provincial furniture and accessories. None had made a connection between her dreams and her home decor. Further, none had connected her dreams to the possibility that she had lived in France during another era.

When I suggested the possibility that past life connections to France could be responsible for their dreams and home decor, each woman was intrigued. In fact, one was so interested that she came to me for a Past Life reading.

I love Japanese gardens, Japanese customs and the country of Japan. Whenever I am exposed to the Japanese culture, I feel a sense of peace and recognition. It is almost like I have gone home.

I believe that this comfort and attraction for anything Japanese reflects a deep soul connection to a prior, pleasant lifetime in Japan. I feel the same way about things related to Ireland. I must have spent at least one happy lifetime in that country.

Clues to past lives can be found in your waking life, as well as in your dreams. Think about the things that you are drawn to, or are repulsed by, in your waking life. All of these things could give you clues about possible past lives.

The following true story illustrates how a waking life incident triggered a boy's past life memories.

A Horse and A Past Life

A woman brought her son to see me because of ongoing nightmares; he was 12 years old at the time. The nightmares had been triggered by an incident that involved a horse.

During a summer holiday, the family decided to go horseback riding. The boy had never before been near horses. Everything was fine until suddenly, her son refused to get on his horse. He became hysterical and started shouting that he didn't want to die by a horse *again*!

Nightmares started shortly after that experience. Visions of death by horses became constant in his dream life. In spite of his distress, he refused to discuss any of it with his parents. The lack of sleep and emotional upheaval, from the nightmares, took their toll. He became exhausted. At that point, they consulted me.

I discussed, with the pair, the possibility that the boy's irrational fear of horses could be due to past life memories. After they grasped the possibility of this, the boy shared the content of his nightmares.

After the sharing, I did a Past Life session with him. It became clear that in one lifetime, at the age of 10, he had been trampled to death by horses. In another lifetime, he died as the result of a broken neck that happened when he fell from a horse.

The regression experience and the information gleaned from it helped him tremendously. He was able to come to terms with his irrational behavior that occurred at the time of the horse riding incident. In addition, he was able to understand and accept the reasons for the horrible visions in his dreams.

The nightmares ceased the night of his consultation with me. Even though he still won't go near horses, he thinks that the "past life stuff is cool!" His mother is still struggling to believe any of it. Nevertheless, she is grateful that the regressions and discussions helped him.

Astral Travel... Are we really doing this or dreaming?

The astral world is a dimension (plane) that exists beyond the physical plane. It is thought to be composed of elements that are light and airy in nature; physical matter doesn't exist there. Similarly, the astral body is diaphanous in nature. It is a duplicate of the physical body, but it is not physical. It exists within the physical body.

Astral travel occurs when the astral body separates from the physical body. The astral body can then move about freely. It can remain in the area around the physical body or go anywhere in the universe. It can travel at the speed of thought. Astral travel is also known as an "out-of-body" experience.

A silver-white, filmy cord connects the two bodies after the astral body has separated from the physical. That cord is the lifeline between the two and it can stretch infinite distances. It is clearly visible to the astral traveler.

Conscious awareness occurs simultaneously in the astral and physical bodies, unless the individual is sleeping. Sometimes, the astral body can temporarily create a duplicate physical body.

During near death experiences, the astral body can leave the physical body. Multiple reports have been written about such events. The "victims" have seen themselves lift out of their physical bodies and float above the accident scene, operating table or other site of their "death". Later, after medical treatment, they could clearly relate conversations and describe events that occurred during the time that they were "dead".

There is an abundance of material written about such experiences. My favorite is the best seller *Life After Life* by Raymond Moody. Another good book is *Life Before Life* by Helen Wambach.

My First Spiritual Flights

The first time I astral traveled was during a sleep-over at a friend's house. I was 13 at the time.

I felt myself lift off the bed and float to the ceiling. I recall that I thought it was a cool dream; yet, at the same time it seemed very strange. I looked down and observed that my friend and I were peacefully sleeping in her bed.

Then, I noticed a wispy, whitish cord extending from my sleeping form to where I was floating near the ceiling. I felt anxious and wasn't sure what was happening. I was curious about the cord and wondered what it was; at the same time, I *knew* that I would be fine.

I heard sounds coming from another room. Before I could finish my thoughts about what or who it could be, I was floating near the kitchen ceiling. I saw my friend's mom and dad conversing with a visitor, over pie and coffee.

I started to feel uneasy. I remember wondering if I was dreaming; it felt so real, yet something was different. I grew more afraid. Suddenly, I was back in my body and asleep.

In the morning I told my friend about the strange dream; she agreed that it was spooky. Then, we went into the kitchen for breakfast.

There, on the counter, were the three cups and plates that I had seen in my "dream". I was stunned. I'd never eaten at my friend's house, thus didn't know what her plates looked like. I looked in the fridge; there was a half eaten pie!

I left for home right after breakfast; I wanted to discuss the dream with my mother. My friend was glad to see me go; she was unnerved by what I had told her. My mother tried to reassure me. She told me that I must have had an unusual dream. At that time, she knew nothing about astral travel.

The second time that I found myself out of my body, I *knew* that I wasn't dreaming. I remember that just prior to the experience I was relaxed, warm and safe in my bed.

Suddenly, I realized that I was floating above my bed. I looked down and saw myself sleeping, with a small smile on my face. Again, I saw a wispy, silver-white cord that was attached to my physical body. That assured me that I was alive and okay. I gave myself permission to rise higher; the cord stretched as I rose. I wondered what was happening.

I recall thinking that I wanted to see my sister. Suddenly, I was in her house watching her sleep. I saw a book, a photograph and a few other items on her night table. I used my thoughts and will, and moved the photograph. Then, I looked around her room and took note of the furnishings and other items. I wanted to be able to tell her what I had seen.

In the next moment, I was back in my bedroom, near the ceiling. Then, I felt my physical body jerk as I re-entered it; it felt a bit like I had fallen.

I don't remember too many details from that astral trip. However, I do remember that things seemed to happen instantaneously.

The next day I called my sister and told her about my dream visit. I was excited and confident. I knew that I could prove that I had visited her. I told her that I had moved the picture. She confirmed that it wasn't in its usual location. She was amazed and a little frightened by my story.

At that time, I didn't know anything about astral travel. Still, I did know that what I'd experienced wasn't a normal dream. Now, I am comfortable with astral traveling. I do it frequently, during my sleeping and waking hours. Sometimes, if the situation warrants, I do it during some of my readings. In those instances, I generally "fly" to gather important information to relay to my clients.

How Risky is Astral Travel?

The whole idea of astral travel may be frightening for you. Let me try to reassure you. I have never heard of it being dangerous; I believe that it is a safe activity. As long as you are alive, the silver, wispy cord will connect your physical and astral bodies. It will guide you back to your physical self.

Some clients have questioned me about the risks of having their cord severed, whether by accident or by some other entity deliberately cutting it. This seems to be a common fear. Let me assure you that it won't happen; I have had direct experience with this.

Once, while I was astral traveling, I saw something pass through my cord. Initially, I was frightened; I thought that I would be disconnected from my physical body. I calmed down when I saw that the thing easily passed through it, just as if the cord was smoke. I discussed the incident with Master Wan Que; he told me that nothing, but a physical death, could sever the connecting cord.

There is another common concern about astral travel, which my clients sometimes discuss with me. That concern is the risk of other spiritual entities inhabiting their physical bodies, while they are out of them. I have never heard of that happening, nor have I experienced it. I do, however, understand the concern.

Part of my preparation, for astral travel, includes setting the intention that the experience will be safe and enlightening. You may wish to do the same. You could call on your angels and guides to protect your astral and physical bodies while they are separated. You could also imagine a white light surrounding and protecting your physical self.

After you have returned from your travels you could visualize a pair of scissors snipping all around your body. The snipping is intended to sever any energetic cords from other beings that may have attached themselves to you. I routinely do this after each "flight".

You may be an astral traveler and not realize it; you simply don't remember your trips. Once you become experienced, you will be more apt to remember your out-of-body experiences. Every trip that you take will increase your confidence. Then, should you wish, you could expand your travel range and visit any place in the cosmos.

If you suspect that you are an astral traveler and don't remember your flights, you could use the scissor exercise every morning or evening to reassure yourself that you alone inhabit your physical form.

The Moon, Dreams and Astral Travel

The moon is associated with the subconscious mind. Thus, the moon may also be closely connected to dreams and astral travel. Some people notice that, during a full moon, their dreams are more vivid, more frequent and more unusual than during the rest of the lunar cycle. I seem to do most of my astral traveling during the week of the full moon.

Tips to Learn How to Astral Travel

It took me several months to learn how to astral travel. I practiced often before I could leave my body at will. Here are some of the things that I learned that may make the process easier:

- First, ensure that you have a genuine desire to astral travel. Then, set the intention that you are able to and will do it. These things are crucial.

- Ensure that you are in a rested and relaxed state; fatigue and stress will impede your ability to leave your body. You may choose to do some slow, deep breathing exercises to help you relax.

🌊 Affirm that astral travel is a safe activity; let go of any fear or worry about leaving your body.

🌊 Visualize where you want to go; begin your journeying by going someplace safe and nearby. After you have mastered traveling short distances, lengthier trips will seem easier.

Some people refer to the targeting of a destination as "astral projection".

🌊 Use your imagination to find creative ways to help you separate from your physical body. I have tried all of the techniques, listed below, with great success.

🌊 Sit in a comfortable chair and visualize yourself floating up to the ceiling. After a few, or perhaps several attempts, you may find yourself floating near the ceiling, looking down at your physical body.

🌊 Visualize a ladder or rope descending from the ceiling to the level of your chest. Reach out to climb the ladder or rope; you may suddenly find yourself out of your body.

🌊 Imagine that your guides or angels are calling you to fly with them.

🌊 Visualize that there is a small plane on your roof and that some one is calling that it's time to take off. You may suddenly find yourself out of your body and in the plane.

🌊 Visualize that Pegasus, the winged horse, is coming to take you for a ride. When you "hear" his hoof beats on the roof, tell him that you are ready to join him. Ask him to wait for a moment until you leave your physical body. Then see yourself on his back, as the two of you take off to explore the cosmos.

Dream Channeling and Messages

Channeling occurs when one energy source uses another to communicate with those in the waking world. This was aptly depicted in the movie Ghost. In that movie, a deceased man's spirit used a medium's body and voice to relay information to his (living) girlfriend.

I have discovered that information and answers to questions can also be channeled through dreams. This is done through the use of inanimate objects.

One technique utilizes a common communications object, such as a pen, paper, phone, computer, book or letter. Focus on the object before going to bed. Mentally ask to be given a message, in your dream, through that object.

You may have to be persistent and go through the ritual several times. Please do not give up. In time, your efforts will very likely be rewarded. Keep in mind that your intention to receive a message is of utmost importance.

I have successfully used this technique several times. Two of those instances are described below:

In the first case, I placed a pencil on my night table and focused on it. After a few moments, I asked my guides for a message. Then, I went to sleep. Please note that I did not ask a question or for an answer.

I repeated my request for four consecutive nights.

On the forth night, I dreamed that I was standing in front of a whiteboard. A felt marker was writing a message on that board.

The message was rich in detail. It was the answer to a problem that I had been pondering over for some time. I was very excited about the whole thing.

A few nights later, I decided to again try the channeling technique. That time I used a phone as the medium object.

I looked at the phone on my night table and affirmed that I needed to hear a message from my guides. I voiced the intent once and mentally repeated it three times, as I lay in bed.

I faithfully repeated the ritual for five nights in a row. On the fifth night, I had a dream in which a phone rang.

I answered the phone and heard a message from my spirit guide, Master Wan Que. He gave me advice on an issue that had been perplexing me. I was amazed and delighted—both with the message and how it had been received.

Do not be surprised if initially you received only written information. Written messages seem to be easier to channel than verbal ones.

The following two exercises, that I developed, may help you to receive messages from your dreams. They are easy to do, please try them.

1. Find a picture that captures your attention. It could be an image of a vintage house or anything else that appeals to you.

Stare at the picture for a few minutes and ask for a message (any kind you like). Alternately, ask for information that you need. Then, remain open to the possibility that the information could come to you in a dream.

You may find that your dream will take you back in time, to the scene in the picture. You may also discover that the message or information that you desired is in that dream scene.

2. Find a photograph of your grandparents, friends or other family members who have passed away. Gaze at the picture before going to sleep.

You may find yourself in the scene or the era of the photograph, in one of your dreams. You may even find yourself interacting with the people in the photograph.

The dream could be lucid. If that occurs, you could ask questions of the individuals from the photograph. You may discover amazing facts about the scene in which you have found yourself.

Keep an open mind; all things are possible!

Conclusion

I hope that this book marks a wonderful and fascinating beginning to your dream consciousness. Or, if you have already begun to work with your dreams, then I hope this book will deepen and broaden your skills.

It is my wish that you experience the beauty and wonder of your dream world. You can fly to magical places in your dreams, if you release all anxiety, worry or fears about the dream world.

Remember, it is your Higher Self who is offering you comfort, love and information while you are in the dream state. Your guides and angels are also trying to lead, support and protect you through your dreams. Answers and enlightenment can be yours, if you decide to study your dreams and act upon the information held in them.

I welcome your comments and questions. I hope that you will share your dream experiences with me. I can be contacted through my website at: **www.irenemartina.com or www.dreamtalk.ca**. Among other things, my website contains inspiring thoughts and dream interpretations.

I look forward to hearing from you.

Blessings,

Irene Martina

Sweet Dreams

About the Author

Insightful and compassionate, Irene is a powerful spiritual counselor, author, speaker and teacher who shares her intuitive gifts and wisdom with a myriad of clients including professionals and non-professionals around the globe.

Irene is the author of *Journey Beyond* and a *Self Discovery Journal* with 366 of her own quotes to inspire you and challenge your spirit to greater self discovery.

She creates her own reading cards through channeled information as well as she has created a Wisdom Deck, Angel Deck and Insight Deck of cards for her many clients to use. Her various readings are unique and original to her and she is recognized for her profound accuracy rate.

Irene has been seen and heard on many television and radio shows and is currently working on a television pilot for her own show.

As a clairvoyant, Irene saw and spoke to her spirit guide when she was four years old; and at the age of eight her dreams started telling her amazing things about her life and opened the doors to the spirit world. She knew she was destined to be something else in life other than an accountant. Irene has a Bachelor of Commerce Degree.

Besides being a clairvoyant and medium, Irene is an NLP (Neuro-Linguistic Practitioner), a certified Adult Training Instructor, Reiki Master and an active member of the Canadian Association of Professional Speakers.

As a professional speaker, Irene speaks on dreams, intuition, meditations, embracing your power, how to discover and awaken your senses and embark on a journey of self discovery. Irene also customizes workshops on these topics.

Irene lives in Edmonton, Alberta and is currently working on a new book and celebrating 30 years of marriage with her best friend and husband, Ron.

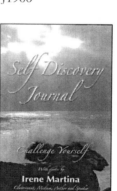